BILL GATES

Ajay Sethi is a Delhi-based writer, with over two and a half decades of writing experience, with publishing credits that include magazine articles, advertising campaigns and commercial and promotional material. An MA English from Delhi University, he has wide reading interests ranging from politics to history and philosophy to religion—a compulsive habit that has also helped to add to his style and content.

THE MAKING OF THE GREATEST
BILL GATES

Ajay Sethi

RUPA

Published by
Rupa Publications India Pvt. Ltd 2019
7/16, Ansari Road, Daryaganj
New Delhi 110002

Sales Centres:
Allahabad Bengaluru Chennai
Hyderabad Jaipur Kathmandu
Kolkata Mumbai

Copyright © Ajay Sethi 2019

The views and opinions expressed in this book are the author's own and the facts are as reported by him which have been verified to the extent possible, and the publishers are not in any way liable for the same.

All rights reserved.
No part of this publication may be reproduced, transmitted, or stored in a retrieval system, in any form or by any means, electronic, mechanical, photocopying, recording or otherwise, without the prior permission of the publisher.

ISBN: 978-93-5333-638-7

Fifth impression 2022

10 9 8 7 6 5

The moral right of the author has been asserted.

Printed in India

This book is sold subject to the condition that it shall not, by way of trade or otherwise, be lent, resold, hired out, or otherwise circulated, without the publisher's prior consent, in any form of binding or cover other than that in which it is published.

Technology is just a tool. In terms of getting the kids working together and motivating them, the teacher is the most important.

— BILL GATES

CONTENTS

Preface	ix
William Henry Gates III	1
Harvard's Most Successful Dropout	9
Byte by Byte	20
Hits and Misses	30
Window(s) to Success	42
The Next Chapter in Tech	58
The Stumbling Blocks	68
'To Whom Much Is Given, Much Is Expected'	81
The Other Founder	89
Mother Mary and the Other Bill Gates	100
Life after Microsoft	106
Epilogue	119
Bibliography	121

PREFACE

A hacker might be the most shocking description of Bill Gates, but it's true! At thirteen, he had hacked his school computer and modified the code to make sure he would be put in a 'class with a disproportionate number of interesting girls'. Then, at fifteen, he hacked the computer of a big corporation. Worse, he is a college dropout and was arrested in 1977 by the Albuquerque, New Mexico police for a traffic violation.

Cut to the present. Gates is the second richest man in the world (overtaken only very recently by Amazon's Jeff Bezos) and is also one of the most large-hearted philanthropists the world has ever seen.

The collage, unusual and interesting as it is, would surely evoke anyone's curiosity to know more about the man, to discover how someone—apparently appearing a bundle of contradictions—was able to follow his childhood dream with a single-minded devotion, unmindful of hurdles and obstacles on the way, meeting any number of challenges and finally making his way to success and glory.

Exciting and interesting as Gates's life story is, it's also inspirational and educative in more ways than one—indeed worth following through.

WILLIAM HENRY GATES III

Don't compare yourself with anyone in this world...
if you do so, you're insulting yourself.
— BILL GATES

The Early Years

Bill Gates was born in Seattle, Washington, on 28 October 1955. His father, William Gates Sr., was a prominent lawyer, and his mother, Mary, was a teacher, community activist and businesswoman. Bill was the second child in the family after his sister Kristianne (Kristi), who was one year older than him. He has another sister, Libby, who is nine years younger. The Gates family were important members of the local Protestant community. Conscious of her duties as a mother, Mary had quit her teaching job earlier, devoting her time mainly to raising family.

Overall, it was a happy and loving family, devoted to Christian values, and caring and supportive of one another. As a child, Bill especially enjoyed non-team events liked roller skating, and later as he grew up, tennis and water skiing. Given their Protestant background, the family encouraged competition—a trait that would stay with Gates for the rest of his life. 'It didn't matter whether it was hearts or pickle ball, or swimming to the dock...there was always a reward for winning, and there was always a penalty for losing,' once a visitor to the family noted.

However, despite all the love and care, certain aspects of Bill's behaviour had started causing concern among his parents as he was growing up. Without any apparent reason, he had begun to withdraw into a shell—becoming more and more quiet and aloof. Sometimes just to check, when his father would call and ask, 'What are you doing?' His reply would be, 'Thinking. Don't you ever think?'

He would be easily bored—and when bored, would need some change. At school he would often get into trouble with other children, and even talk back to his teachers. He was generally struggling in life. His parents had started getting worried about his behaviour and feared he might become a loner. His father decided to consult a counsellor. After a few sessions, the counsellor too didn't sound too hopeful. He said to his father that there was no use trying to force him to conform. 'You're going to lose. You had better adjust.'

They thus sought to channelize his energies in positive productive directions. They made him participate in boy scout activities (he even earned his Eagle Scout badge) and also encouraged him to take part in team sports. They were happy to discover his growing interest in reading and so fuelled his curiosity further through science fiction books. These steps worked to improve matters and things began to change.

New School Helps Him to Blossom

When he was thirteen, Gates was admitted to an exclusive upscale Lakeside School in Seattle. Although his family was a supporter of the public education system, they felt this new school would challenge him and help him to blossom. And blossom he did! A certain turn of events here gave a new direction to his life, tapped into his hidden talents, and brought out the best in him. He met Paul Allen, two years his senior, and despite differences in personalities, struck a great friendship with him. What brought the two together was their love of computers. Being an intelligent child and good in math, he had developed an inclination towards the machine, which was quite a novelty those days. Here, the Mother's Club of the school had used proceeds from the school's rummage sale to buy a teletype terminal for students to have familiarity with the computer. Bill, being a natural in this environment, felt quite at home in the computer room. This was his calling. He would find it difficult to tear himself from the machine. He later wrote, 'There's something neat about the machine... It was hard to tear myself away from a machine at which I could so unambiguously demonstrate success.' Both he and Paul had become quite passionate about computers.

Paul Allen would often dress up in a sports coat and a tie, and carry a leather briefcase, and bus it down to the local computer gurus' offices in search of discarded code. While codes would be easily available to the employees of the companies, Paul and Bill had to hunt for it. Allen would boost a smaller Bill into dumpsters and they would get 'these coffee-stained texts (of computer code) from behind the offices'. Once, they even found the printout of an important source code that unlocked a lot of secrets.

A result of these efforts was that around this time, Bill was able to develop a programme called Tic-Tac-Toe, in BASIC computer language, which allowed users to play games against the computer—and later, another one, Traf-O-Data, along with Paul, to make traffic counters based on an Intel 8008 processor. In their childish enthusiasm, once when they even hacked a Computer Centre Corporation computer to get extra time on it. They were reprimanded for it and also banned for four weeks from using the computer.

That's how life was when they were together at Lakeside. Soon, all this was about to change. As Paul was two years ahead of him, he left and went on to join Washington State University. Bill was to follow later. Life had too many surprises in store for them.

Early Influences

Children learn from their environment, especially from elders at home and school. Impressions and influences in formative years play a major role in later life. In case of Bill, this was particularly so, as he was fortunate to be guided by some very strong individuals, very rooted in their ethics and positive values.

Bill's father had a profound impact on the young boy. His father's lessons stayed with him and deeply impacted his personality. His father often said:

- Having diverse interests and hobbies is a good thing, but those interests shouldn't be pursued at the expense of important family commitments.
- It is important to show solidarity with the community, even if it's for small causes — for collecting funds for slum rehabilitation, or

helping a neighbour clear his driveway in the event of a storm.
- Always playing safe in life is not an option—learn to get out of your comfort zone, give yourself to new experiences and undertake new experiments. Even if you fail, you would come away with a bagful of lessons, which will stand you in good stead in the years to come.
- A balance is necessary between the indoors and outdoors, between classroom teaching and practical life.
- To expand your horizon, stay curious and learn more about things around yourself.
- Those blessed with means should try to help out others as much as they can, following the lesson from the Book of Luke, New Testament, 'To whom much is given, (from him) much is expected.'

Among Bill's earliest influences were some strong women as well, whose ideas and thoughts guided him from an early age. These include his mother and his maternal grandmother.

Gates said in a Harvard commencement speech about his mother, 'She never stopped pressing me to do more for others.' In this context, he has also talked of a letter his mother had written to his fiancée Melinda in 1993, a little before his marriage, where her advice echoed Voltaire's belief that with great power comes great responsibility. We must recall that around this time, Gates was one of the wealthiest people in the world, and his mother expected him and his wife to do much for others.

Mrs Blanche Caffiere—Friend, Philosopher and Guide

Gates has also singled out one of his earliest teachers, Mrs Blanche Caffiere, a librarian in Seattle's View Ridge Elementary school, for special mention, as one who had a big influence on him. When he was a 'timid fourth grader,' she drew him out of his shell, and she, with her knowledge about books, fuelled his interest in different types of reading.

'Mrs Caffiere took me under her wing and helped make it okay for me to be a messy, nerdy boy, who was reading lots of books,' said Gates.

She would often start with questions like, 'What do you like to read?' and 'What are you interested in?' She gave him great biographies she had read. She would genuinely listen to what he had to say. 'Through those book conversations in the library and in the classroom, we became good friends,' said Gates.

Mrs Caffiere died in 2006, shortly after her 100th

birthday. Before she passed away, Gates had an opportunity to thank her for the important role she had played in his life, '...stoking my passion for learning at a time when I easily could have gotten turned off by school.'

HARVARD'S MOST SUCCESSFUL DROPOUT

> *I failed in some subjects in (an) exam,*
> *but my friend passed in all. Now he's an engineer*
> *in Microsoft and I am the owner of Microsoft.*
> —BILL GATES

Life at Harvard

For most people, getting into Harvard is a dream. It's the opening up of new avenues and opportunities. While for Gates too, it was not any different, he was looking for something beyond what Harvard had to offer. And given his determination and vision, it was to show up soon.

A math prodigy who was in love with computers, Gates was ready to paint a larger canvas of his own life at the time of leaving school. When he graduated from the Lakeside School in Seattle, he was a National Merit Scholar, having scored 1590 out of 1600 on the Scholastic Aptitude Tests (more commonly known as SATs) in 1973.

Given his exceptional school credits, his entry into Harvard in 1973 was rather easy, and there he not only opted for pre-law major, but also took mathematics and graduate-level computer science courses. Although he chose law, as his father was an eminent lawyer and the family was keen on his joining the profession, his interest lay elsewhere.

As computers were his first love, at Harvard too he was driven by programming and he used this opportunity to spend as much time as possible on the school's computers. 'I used to sit in a lot of classes that I hadn't even signed up for,' he later recalled in his 2007 Harvard Commencement Speech. Harvard was a 'phenomenal experience' for him. 'Academic life was fascinating,' he said. According to him, it was an extraordinary experience to be 'amidst so much of energy and intelligence… It could be exhilarating, intimidating, sometimes even discouraging, but always challenging. It was an amazing privilege and though I left early, I was transformed by my years at Harvard.'

At Harvard again, he was less in his classes and more in the computer room. Although Paul had left school two years before him, Gates had kept in touch. Without him, he felt a little handicapped and was keen that the two resume their collaborative projects. 'We were each other's soundboards,' Paul had said in an interview later. After leaving school, Paul had joined Washington University, but on Bill's persuasion he left after two years and joined Honeywell near Boston. Being near to each other, the two could now pursue their dreams together. Bill remembers, they would call big companies and ask for programming assignments, and their reply would be, 'You guys are just high-school kids...We do that work ourselves.'

Baby Steps in Business

On a frigid December afternoon, as Paul was crossing the Harvard Yard, he chanced upon the January 1975 edition of the electronics journal, *Popular Electronics*. It had a picture of the kit of Altair 8800, a new microcomputer, on the cover, with the caption: 'Project Breakthrough, World's first Microcomputer Kit to rival commercial models (save over $1,000).'

Paul grabbed the copy and ran to Bill and suggested to him that they develop a programme for this simple little machine. Altair 8800 was not the first microcomputer, but it was the first to catch people's imagination. Economically priced, it was a big draw among computer enthusiasts. The computer didn't look like much, just a rectangular box with several rows of tiny toggle switches across the front and no software, disk drive or keyboard. The buyer had to assemble it from a kit. As against the modern personal computer (PC) that has 8 million bytes today, it had just 256 bytes.

This was to be their big project together, though they had been collaborating on software projects earlier. In fact, now, excited as Paul was by the prospect of 'adopting' the machine, he kept telling Bill, 'Let's start a company. Let's do it.' Commenting on the episode later, Bill had remarked, 'We realized the revolution might happen without us. After we saw the article, there was no question of where our life would focus.'

Micro Instrumentation and Telemetry Systems's (MITS) co-founder, Ed Roberts, had earlier told them, 'We are getting about ten letters a day from people... I'd tell them whoever writes it first, gets the job.' Subsequently, as they got the go-ahead on the project, their next challenge was how and where to write the programme as they didn't have an Altair 8800. Despite this handicap, they found a solution and decided to use the Harvard computers for the job. For the next six weeks, Gates was like a possessed man. During this time, he almost lived at Harvard. Unmindful of rest, sleep or food, he got down to the job at a furious pace. Grabbing a meal here or there, he would take a nap in a corner or would even dose off on the keyboard. As Paul was at Honeywell nearby, he would come regularly to assist and contribute his bit. They even hired some other Harvard students to assist them in small jobs. Many bugs were fixed later.

Their programme was soon ready, but they didn't have the right machine to test it. They had no option but to give the maiden demonstration right at MITS. Finally, it was decided that Paul would go, as in appearance he looked mature enough to handle important projects. He flew to Albuquerque for the presentation. Destiny was as if favouring them. The programme worked perfectly on the company's machine and the company accepted their product. 'I called Bill, and said it worked,' says Paul. 'We were over the moon.' Paul celebrated the success by treating himself to an extra large pizza. As their product was accepted, it resulted in a deal with the company, which agreed to distribute the machine as Altair BASIC, virtually accepting their imprint on it.

Paul was offered a job at the company, which he accepted. Gates took leave of absence from Harvard, telling his parents that he would go back if things didn't work out. This first major break had boosted their confidence and they decided to form a company, though their foray into business was far from easy. Both he and Paul Allen spent a lot of time questioning themselves and their decision to risk everything and chase their dream. Perhaps destiny was nudging them towards this path as, around this time, an exciting opportunity presented itself before them.

They named their venture 'Micro-Soft' (a combination of 'microcomputer' and 'software') and continued to work under the aegis of MITS. However, within a year, towards the end of 1976, they became independent of MITS. The hyphen was dropped, and on 26 November 1976, the trade name 'Microsoft' was registered in New Mexico in the United States.

As their company began to grow, Gates felt no reason to go back to Harvard to get his degree. From now on, they continued to develop programming software for a variety of systems and companies. Later, on 1 January 1979, they moved their headquarters to Bellevue, Washington.

IBM Deal—the Turning Point

Some people called it the 'Deal of the Century.' And others, 'Deal with the Devil.'

Although, given his intelligence and drive, Gates was sure to be successful in his endeavours sooner or later, at this time, destiny appeared to be favouring him. The Altair success had brought them some basic recognition and had started getting them other assignments, but it was the International Business Machines Corporation

HARVARD'S MOST SUCCESSFUL DROPOUT

(or as it is more popularly known—IBM) deal that was to be the biggest breakthrough of it all. It happened five years after their launching of Microsoft.

At the time of the IBM deal, Microsoft was a five-year-old company, run by two very young entrepreneurs. In the summer of 1980, Gates was just twenty-four and Paul had turned twenty-seven. As Gates looked younger than his age, people in the professional world often got confused about his exact role and position. There goes a story that once a member of the negotiating team took him to be a secretary and asked him to get coffee. That apart, the MITS connection had given them some basic recognition and they had started getting programming contracts for different companies.

Around this time, many computer companies—both established and start-ups—had begun to toy with the idea of producing smaller computers for the personal use of individuals. IBM remained the Big Blue, the colossus dominating the entire computer landscape. And as the buzz in favour of the smaller computers had started growing, IBM didn't want to lose out on the opportunity. It created a separate division for the development of PCs. In the summer of 1980, the company had developed a system, IBM PC, for which they needed an operating system (O/S). By some oversight, in IBM's 'briefing books,' Microsoft was listed as a major developer of O/S, so IBM decided to try them out and requested for an O/S for their new PC.

As the description of 'major developer of operating system' didn't quite fit their venture, Gates was a little surprised by the request. Gates's mother knew John Opel of IBM, who had served with her on the same board of United Way Charity (UWC) of America, and Microsoft was hoping to sell BASIC and other languages with the new IBM microcomputer. When this request for an O/S came from IBM, Gates was quite confused to say the least. Gary Kildall of Intergalactic Digital Research (IDR), who was an established figure in the field of microcomputers, had written the Control Program for Microcomputers (more commonly known as CP/M), a mass-market O/S that was ideally suited for the IBM PC. So, Gates referred the IBM people to him.

Somehow things didn't go well between IBM and IDR. There are different versions about it — it's said that Kildall's wife was rather stand-offish, and by the time the IBM team arrived at his residence, Kildall had gone away for his morning air-trip in his plane. Another story says that he did arrive around lunch time, but instead of an outright sale, Kildall asked for $10 per copy. In short, the negotiations didn't work out. Following these developments, Gates decided to explore other options as he didn't want to lose out on the other business he was hoping to get from IBM. He promised IBM an O/S.

HARVARD'S MOST SUCCESSFUL DROPOUT

There's a certain background as to how and why Gates promised IBM the O/S. Actually, Paul knew one Tim Patterson at Seattle Computer Products (SCP) who had been working on an alternative version of CP/M — he called it QDOS (short for Quick and Dirty O/S). Microsoft suggested to IBM that they could buy this software and further work on it to suit the IBM PC. As they agreed to it, after the signing of the contract with IBM, Microsoft bought the software from SCP. Gates and Allen worked on it to suit the IBM requirement. It was approved, and finally the product was ready for shipping towards the end of 1981. The PC was to be named IBM PC-DOS.

Now, we have a twist in the tale. Although it appeared to be a regular deal, it turned out to be much more for Microsoft in the long run. Besides being a gifted software talent, Gates also had a shrewd business sense. It's said that perhaps Gates Sr.'s years of drafting contracts for companies also came in handy here. In the contract with IBM, a clause was cleverly added that allowed the company to sell the same O/S to other companies too under the name MS-DOS (short for Microsoft Disk O/S). It was this one line that changed the course of the entire computer industry and made Gates and Allen the richest people in the world. In addition to a licence fee per IBM machine, Microsoft was free to sell the same O/S to other manufacturers.

In the words of Bill Gates, around that time, the companies didn't think much of the software. In many cases, it came free with the equipment. For most, hardware was the thing. Gates said that the companies didn't realize that eventually software would be bigger than hardware. It was this mindset at the time due to which IBM didn't pay much heed to the seemingly 'harmless' clause. However, it set off a chain reaction that helped in revolutionizing the IT industry and bringing the computer into every home.

The IBM PC was the first major PC to hit the market, and as its popularity increased, competition was quick to take notice of the development and keen to take advantage of the situation. For a host of companies, it could be a gold mine—they started on the reverse engineering and were soon ready with an IBM clone. Now, as they wanted an O/S for it, Microsoft was quick at hand to supply one. It's reported that Compaq was the first to reverse-engineer the PC. Established in 1982, during its second year of operation, it was able to sell 53,000 PCs, hitting a sale of $111 million. In 1987, it hit the $1 billion mark, taking the shortest time to reach there. Then there were companies like Dell, Hewlett-Packard and others. Demand from all these had begun to add to Microsoft's sale.

In retrospect, after the IBM deal, there was no looking back for Microsoft. The IBM connection gradually propelled them into the big league and big money. If Microsft's revenue was $16,005 in 1976, in a short span of seven years it had grown to $55 million in 1983, and it stands at $125.8 billion as of June 2019. In over four decades of its existence, the company has traversed an interesting and long journey—it has had its share of ups and downs, and successes and failures, but overall, has continued to show a great degree of resilience and generally delivering better-than-expected results. What has made it a formidable market player and a dominant tech force needs closer analysis and scrutiny.

But first, some glimpses into the background conditions of the world and computer industry then, which made all this possible.

BYTE BY BYTE

Life is not fair, get used to it. We all need people who will give us feedback. That's how we improve.
—BILL GATES

Growth of the Computer Industry and the Arrival of the Internet

After the Industrial Revolution of the 17th–18th centuries, the world had grown on the back of traditional manufacturing and service industries. So the rich list of the world contained names who owned tangible assets—real estate, factories, superstores, etc. But with the convergence of technologies, the world had started to become a different place and, in time, was set to undergo a paradigm shift. In our context here, since the issue is connected with the growth of the IT industry and the life of Bill Gates, the subject calls for a detailed analysis. Let's have a closer look.

After 1950, the world was set to be transformed on account of many major factors. First of all, owing to large-scale devastation during the World War II and the end of colonial rule, large parts of the world needed to be rebuilt. This had spurred industrial and manufacturing activity in the West, and especially in the US, on an unprecedented scale. Secondly, after the fall of the Berlin Wall in 1989, the world had started to become a smaller place with markets opening up all over. And finally, with some major advances in the previous years, the computer industry had taken a few quantum leaps, and was set to become the dominant technology of the future. So, after the 1980s, all these factors combined together were going to make the world a very different place and even redefine the way modern empires would be built and fortunes made.

To understand how such events had begun to impact and change the lives of individuals and entities, let's first have a look at the history of computers, discover how it has evolved over time, and how things stood in this respect around 1950. Interestingly, some of the greatest inventions in history have been the result of trying circumstances, especially wars. In recent times, the World Wars have spurred some of the biggest inventions, which have had a huge impact on standards of living. If World

War I served as a test bed for the development of the airplane and its use as a warcraft, World War II brought us the helicopter and digital electronic computer.

Manual and mechanical computing devices had existed since ancient times. From the abacus in about 500 BCE, there had been progress towards mechanical analogue computers in the medieval Islamic world in the 11th–12th centuries. Later, with the advent of electricity in the early 20th century, it became possible to develop electrically driven mechanical analogue computers. By 1912, Arthur Pollen, a leading British journalist and businessman, was able to produce one of the world's first electrically powered analogue computers, patented as the Argo Clock.

It was around this time that IBM was set up in the US. The earlier name of IBM was the Computing-Tabulating-Recording company (CTR) when it was set up in 1911 in Endicott, New York, as a holding company of manufacturers of record-keeping and measuring systems. It was later named as International Business Machines in 1924. It was IBM that supplied analogue computers to assist in the building of the first atom bomb, and later the first digital electronic computer was developed in the University of Pennsylvania and dedicated to the nation on 14 February 1946. Called ENIAC (short for Electronic Numerical Integrator and Computer), its development was necessitated by the need to calculate firing tables for artillery. It weighed 60,000 pounds, covered an area of 1,800 sq. ft. and had cost about $487,000, which was a phenomenal sum those days. After the war, ENIAC was mainly used to carry out calculations related to the production of the hydrogen bomb.

Following this, in early 1950s, there came a big push to the development of nuclear and space sciences, and consequently to digital electronic computers, as they were critical to their growth and advancement. Perhaps it would not have been possible for man to achieve the moon landing in 1969 had it not been for the advancements in IT. Undeniably, most major human endeavours are marked by the desire to push the envelope. 'What next?' is the perpetual question.

In the late 1960s, a feeling had started growing in the industry as how to further improve and harness computer technology for the larger good of mankind. Scientists had even started wondering whether it was possible to put the computer on the desk to aid people in their day-to-day activities. As research was taking place in different areas of electronics, it was actually the advancement in the microprocessor technology that made this possible.

Microprocessor—the Game Changer

The radio of yore was a big bulky device that would occupy the whole table. Its big size was essentially on account of the large vacuum tubes that performed the function of controlling and relaying the electrical current. These tubes had existed since the beginning of the century, and were used in practically all electrical devices. Subsequent researches in the field, for an improvement on these, led to the invention of the transistor in 1948, which was a major step forward. However, what totally changed the electronic landscape was the integration of a large number of transistors on a small flat metal piece (first geranium and later silicon), called the integrated circuit (ASIC, or simply IC).

Some early attempts were made in this direction around the late 1940s. In 1949, Werner Jacobi, a scientist working in Siemens, had filed for a patent for an early version of IC in 1949, which had only five transistors. It was a nascent idea that couldn't be fully implemented. More serious attempts were made in the late '50s with scientists like Jack Kilby, Robert Noyce, Kurt Lehovec, Jean Hoerni and some others taking the lead.

As there were conflicting claims as to who actually invented the IC and a patent war ensued, the American press later narrowed the list to Jack Kilby and Robert Noyce. Kilby was later awarded the Noble Prize in

Physics in 2000 for his 'contribution to the development of IC.' The IC paved the way for the development of the microprocessor, which is the heart—the controlling unit—of a computer or machine. An IC forms the basis of a microprocessor that may contain more than one IC.

Over time, the convergence of technologies had continued to bring us more advanced and sophisticated products. So, when the scientists were able to integrate a large number of transistors on a single chip, it was considered a major breakthrough of the time; but as yet, few had realized the enormous possibilities it was about to open up for mankind. Another major fallout of these developments was that it became possible to produce chips on a mass scale, which meant lowering of cost.

The increasing powers of the microprocessor, and consequently its mass production, were set to change the entire landscape of technology, and in turn, the future of mankind. In time, microprocessor-backed technology would impact every field of human activity—from automobile to aviation, agriculture to education, medicine to nuclear, and space sciences to printing and publishing. Computerized devices would be found everywhere, ranging from people's homes to high-end nuclear facilities.

An overview of the progress of the microprocessor gives us an idea about its increased power and capability over time. While Intel's first-generation microprocessor, the 4004, had 2,300 transistors, the later versions continued to improve on the earlier ones, with the 8080 in 1974 having 6,000 transistors, the 8085 in 1976 with 6,500 transistors and so on. The Intel Pentium IV released in year 2000 contained 42 million transistors.

In short, with every passing year the companies have continued to make microprocessors faster and more powerful. The difference between the earlier and later versions is mainly the speed — the advanced microprocessors can perform millions of tasks per second, and quickly move data between various memory locations.

Thus, the stage was set for phenomenal growth in the computer industry, especially the PC (as it has a mass market). It was also the time for talent to seize the opportunity.

While young entrepreneurs with no previous experience but only passion and drive, like Bill Gates, Paul Allen, Steve Jobs and Michael Dell, had ventured out into the field, industry veterans like Gordon Moore and Robert Noyce of Intel also entered the market. This meant increasing competition. Intel was established in 1968, SAP in 1972, Microsoft in 1975, Apple in 1976, Oracle in 1977, Sun Microsystems and Adobe in 1982, and Dell and Cisco in 1984.

Next Wave—the Internet

If the early '50s and '60s were the era of large computers and mainframes, and the late '70s a period marked by a growth in microcomputers and PCs, the early '90s saw a totally new dimension being added to the IT industry. A standalone computer is just a sophisticated typewriter, or a video or gaming device, but once connected to other computers, it assumes a different character and becomes a node in a large chain. Efforts were being made since the early '60s to produce some kind of network that would facilitate messaging and graphic and text transmission from one machine to another. The early attempts included projects like the Advanced Research Projects Agency Network (ARPANET), the NPL (short for National Physical Laboratory) Network, Telenet and others.

However, the real breakthrough came with the creation of the World Wide Web (WWW), developed by the British scientist Tim Berners-Lee, while conducting research at CERN Switzerland in the early '80s. This development made the linking of different computers possible, wherein the network could be accessible from any node. With its further development in the '90s, a new world—electronic messaging, voice mail, video interface, Internet—opened up like never before. If the railways and aviation were the major connectors for humanity earlier, the Internet has proved to be the next big thing.

The Internet involves interconnected software or hardware storage devices called servers, which contain all the content, web pages and sites uploaded onto them from time to time, and to which individual computers (or nodes) can get connected, share the data and services, and download or upload files. After the early '90s, the Net continued to grow exponentially, which meant more and more servers got linked to it, and millions of pages and sites got added to it.

Such was the environment in which computer companies had begun to vie with one another for a bigger and bigger share of the computer pie. One point to note here is, every individual (or entity) has his 'forte'; he can't be the master of all. So, interestingly, as the computer industry began to expand, there came to be a greater need of coordination and cooperation between the competing entities. If IBM was the big boy of hardware, it needed to buy the O/S from Microsoft; while Intel was the master of the computer chip, it needed Apple to drive its sale. So, while on one side they were competing in the market, on the other, they needed each other. Interdependence was the name of the game.

Hence, what began in the US in the '80s and '90s and gradually spread across the world, would, in the coming decades, become a race extremely exciting, and even unexpected at times. Some companies would be gobbled up by the bigger fish (IBM's purchase of Lotus), others might drop out of the contention (Hotmail selling off to Microsoft), while some others would continue to become bigger and bigger (Apple, Microsoft, IBM, Facebook, Amazon, etc.) and even get embroiled in monopoly issues.

HITS AND MISSES

*Your most unhappy customers are
your greatest source of learning.*
—BILL GATES

Success and Growth of Microsoft

The fact that even after over four decades of fierce competition and 'tech wars', Microsoft continues to be one of the largest computer companies in the world has a lot to do with the drive and vision of one man: Bill Gates. It was the genius of Gates that could spot the opportunity, make the right move at the right time and turn things to his advantage. In other words, he had a finger on the pulse of the market and was able to offer a product that would have 'wide acceptance' and 'wide applicability'. Once the product was accepted by the people, he would ensure its repeat purchase, by dealing with the competition on one hand, and ensuring product improvement through constant enhancements and upgradations, on the other.

Till today, the Windows O/S and Microsoft Office remain some of the most sought-after programmes ever—and among the major revenue earners for the company. As they remain the company's 'jewels in the crown', the story of their growth and development calls for a comprehensive analysis, which takes us through the various developments and modifications they have gone through over time, and their current position therein.

However, looking at the general growth of the company, to begin with we need to focus on the period from 1975-95, as it remains the most important phase in the history of Microsoft. This was a period marked by success, growth and consolidation. During this time, the company had been able to establish its supremacy in certain areas and would remain practically unchallenged in those in the future. Although after the '90s, it kept making forays into other areas, like hardware, gaming consoles, artificial intelligence (AI), and later also cloud computing and PC hardware, for quite some time, upgradations and enhancements related to Windows and MS Office occupied the company's energies. It's only after 2000 that other products began to come into prominence. Since the first twenty-five years have remained the main foundation years, let's first examine this period in detail.

We know that after the success of MS-DOS in 1981, the company had got the resources to begin an era of expansion and consolidation. What further boosted the company's finances was the fact that IBM again approached them in 1985 for the development of an O/S for their next version. As was the case with the earlier MS-DOS (developed in 1981), this time again Microsoft continued to sell its own version of the new software in the market, which would later overshadow the IBM OS/2 and further improve Microsoft's revenue.

As the era of innovation had begun, one major feature introduced during this time was graphical user interface (GUI), which would become a permanent fixture of the PC environment. It was developed by Microsoft under the supervision of Bill Gates for Apple Computers and was later used in Windows 85. Apple took it to be an infringement of their patent rights, but later the matter was settled out of court. While earlier, the PC screen would only show the typed text, with the introduction of graphic icons, a certain richness and variety were added to the operation. It also freed the user from keyboard-command and allowed him to access files and data, using a mouse to click on 'graphic' icons. It was to be a new 'window' of experience for him—thus, the name stuck and later became a household name.

HITS AND MISSES

Starting 1985, MS-DOS, in the new avatar of Windows, with additional features like GUI, would be set on a course that would be unstoppable in the history of computers. From 1985 till now, about twenty-six Windows versions for the PC, besides others for servers and devices, have been released, the details of which have been discussed in a separate chapter.

Another major innovation during this period that improved the company's prospects in the long run was the development of Office applications—first Word, then Excel, and finally PowerPoint. To begin with, all these applications had been developed at different times, and continued to be sold as separate products. Word was released for DOS in 1983 and for Mac in 1985; Excel for Mac in 1985 and for Windows in 1987; and PowerPoint for Mac in 1987 and for Windows in 1990. Although they had been selling well individually and had good market share, it's only when their integration happened—first in a common package called Microsoft Office and later in the early '90s with the Windows— that the whole Windows package became an unbeatable product.

Around 1984, an IT magazine, *InfoWorld* (2 April 1984), had stated,

> Microsoft is widely recognized as the most influential company in (the) microcomputer

software industry. Claiming more than a million installed MS-DOS machines, (the) founder and chairman... has decided to certify MS's jump on the rest of the industry by dominating applications, operating systems, peripherals, and most recently book publishing. Some insiders say MS is attempting to be the IBM of (the) software industry.

Growth beyond 1995

We're aware that right from the beginning, one of the biggest advantages of Microsoft had been the stupendous success of Windows. On the back of Windows, it could afford to experiment, innovate, expand, diversify and even take risks and afford to fail. Windows gave it the financial muscle to power its way ahead into the fiercely growing competitive market. In this respect, a rather unflattering term was developed by some writers, 'Embrace, Extend, Extinguish,' outlining Microsoft's general strategy of growth. The company would look for a fledgling product in the market, adopt it, change or modify it to suit its own needs and then make it its own, and 'extinguish' the earlier product. In a 2008 interview, Steve Ballmer, CEO Microsoft, said that the company's policy was to continue to pursue 'new technologies even if initial attempts fail.' He gave the example of Windows, which Microsoft has continued to update and refine over time.

So, the growing revenue had opened up many new vistas of opportunities and possibilities for the company. It was able to hire new talent, invest in research and development, and enhance and expand its product range. As the company had already got a grip on the O/Ss and Office applications for PCs, its future policy was to follow a twin-fold objective: Firstly, not to loosen its grip on Windows and MS Office by ensuring complete customer satisfaction through upgradations and improvements, and secondly, compete with full might of technology and money power in other areas to get ahead.

Around 2000, the IT industry had started growing at an unprecedented rate on the back of a spurt in manufacturing and services activities round the globe—countries like China and India, with large markets, had started recording 7-8 per cent growth, becoming new engines of world growth. The fast pace of growth had necessitated the need for all kinds of IT products, ranging from computers to peripherals, custom software and servers to shared services facilities. The growth of the Internet was perhaps the biggest contributing factor to this increased demand.

One major positive fallout of the Internet was the general growth of email. It was believed around that time, that 80 per cent of the use of Internet was for emails. Microsoft's acquisition of Hotmail in 1997 for $500 million for those times was an expensive buy, but a strategic one. While the company kept on upgrading its Windows and Office offerings, it didn't lose sight of the general developments in the market. In 1995, Gates issued an 'Internet Tidal Wave Memo', which outlined the company's strategy in view of the new developments in the IT field. It called for a renewed thrust in the networking and WWW space. Microsoft's MSN was originally intended to be a competitor to the Internet.

All this was in sync with Bill Gates's policy. He had always been alive to the market conditions, and the competitive threats arising therein. Although software was their strength, they wouldn't like to lag behind in the hardware and services areas. The company was among the first to introduce the GUI mouse with Windows. In the mid-90s when Internet entered the scene, Microsoft was quick to launch its own web browser, the Internet Explorer (IE). It had stiff competition in Netscape, but was able to deal with it smartly. In 1996, Microsoft collaborated with the National Broadcasting Company (NBC) to create a 24/7 cable news channel called MSNBC.

In view of all these developments, after 2000, Microsoft's thrust came to be in four main areas (apart from the Windows and MS Office products). These included the video-game consoles market, cloud computing services, mobile phones, and tablets and PCs branded as Surface.

Always interested in the video-game console market, Microsoft released Xbox in the end of 2001. The market, around that time, was dominated by Sony and Nintendo. Later, an improved version of the Xbox was released in November 2005 called Xbox360. The gaming console offered two versions: a basic version for $299.9 and a 'bells and whistles' version for $399.99.

To deal with the growing IT services market competition, the Azure Services Platform was released on 27 October 2008, which heralded the company's entry into the cloud computing service market. It offers to clients on demand all kinds of IT services through the company-managed data centres. It was announced in October 2008, with the codename 'Project Red Dog', and was subsequently released in 2010 as Windows Azure. It later became Microsoft Azure in 2014. Given the competition and more and more players entering the arena, the company needed the extra push to make a place for itself. But over time, as its efforts have begun to pay off, it hopes to become a major player in the field in the coming time.

The next big step for Microsoft was the establishing of a chain of retail stores named Microsoft Store, to sell their products. The first store was opened in 2009 in Scottsdale in Arizona.

The launch of smartphones saw the company enter the market with its O/Ss. Although BlackBerry was a precursor to the 'smart phone', the device came into its own in 2007 with many improved versions, with LG introducing LG Prada, and later, Apple launching the iPhone. To begin with, Microsoft made determined efforts to capture the smartphone O/S market. It sought to revamp its aging mobile O/S, Windows mobile, and was able to replace it with Windows Phone O/S. To consolidate its position in the mobile market, it acquired Nokia's mobile unit in 2013 for $7 billion. In the PC and tablet market it made its entry by launching the Surface range of PCs in October 2012. For the company, it was a major event and shift in policy as its Surface range of PCs had hardware made by Microsoft itself, and was supported by Windows 8.

One important childhood lesson that Gates had learnt and which had become part of the company's philosophy was that one shouldn't be afraid to make mistakes; on the contrary, one should learn from them. Even if the company was not able to make much headway in one area, it was still worth trying. It would learn from the effort and plod on.

With respect to mobile phones and their O/S, and PC and tablet hardware, there had been much competition in the market and they remained Microsoft's weak areas. On 19 July 2013, the company stocks took a first major hit since 2000, due to the poor showing of both Windows 8 and the Surface tablet. Over $32 billion was wiped off Microsoft's market capitalization. Again, there was never very encouraging news on the mobile phone front. The company's share in the US smartphone market was a measly 2.7 per cent in January 2016. In early 2015, Microsoft had lost $7.6 billion owing to a drop in demand in its mobile business, and this led to the sacking of 7,800 employees.

However, the good news for Microsoft is that in addition to Windows, which has been its strong point till now, Microsoft has been able to make its mark in new technology areas like cloud computing, Azure Services Platform and the gaming consoles business. In 2018, Azure's market share grew from 14 per cent to 16 per cent, while gaming product Xbox's revenue has been steadily growing, recording 39 per cent growth in 2018. The company has continued to explore newer avenues and expand in other areas. In a project named 'Azure Government,' it has partnered with seventeen American Intelligence agencies to develop products that track American citizens. It has also developed special equipment for the army, called the Microsoft HoloLens headsets, which enhance troops' capability to engage with the enemy by the high-power detection of their movements.

One business policy often followed by ambitious companies is, either develop a good product yourself, or buy a successful product and make it your own. That's the general trend the computer industry had been following beyond the '90s. As a consequence, many early competitors of Microsoft had disappeared as they were either bought by other larger companies or crushed by Microsoft itself. But then others kept showing up, keeping Microsoft on its toes. IBM bought Lotus in 1995 in an attempt to compete with Windows, and Oracle acquired Sun Microsystems in 2010 to strengthen its Unix-based software ecosystem. Novell was crushed by Microsoft in 1995.

Mergers and Acquisitions

Ever since its public offering in 1986, Microsoft has, in all, acquired 225 companies, bought stakes in sixty-four, and has made twenty-five disinvestments. Of these acquisitions, 107 companies were based in the US. In its initial years, it made some major acquisitions that included Forethought, the creator of PowerPoint in 1987, and Hotmail in 1997 for $500 million. Some of its key acquisitions since then include: Flash Communications in 1997, NetGames in 2000, Visio Corporation in 1999 (for $1.3 billion), Nokia in 2013 (for $7.2 billion), Skype in 2011 (for $8.5 billion),

HITS AND MISSES

GitHub in 2018 (for $7.5 billion), and LinkedIn in 2016 (for $28.1 billion).

In its 1989 financial report, the company had listed two types of competitors: In the software category, IBM, AT&T and Apple; and among the independent systems software vendors, Digital Research and AT&T. Although the company had made some forays into hardware by introducing the mouse with the 1983 MS-DOS, it was yet not a serious player in any of those categories, while the major competitors were vertically integrated. However, in its long journey of over four decades, the picture has changed considerably and today it presents quite a varied product profile after venturing out into new areas and through mergers and acquisitions. Though Windows and MS Office still continue to be Microsoft's major market strengths, its competitors have continued to change over time, and currently it has Apple, IBM, Amazon and Google as its main rivals.

WINDOW(S) TO SUCCESS

I choose a lazy person to do a hard job — because a lazy person will find an easy way to do it.
— BILL GATES

Windows & MS Office

As Windows and MS Office are Microsoft's major offerings, we need to analyse their growth and development in detail. First of all, let's look at the reasons for the success of Windows and MS Office. We know that Linux too had been in direct competition with Windows a few years later, and as it was 'open source' and thus free, it should've been preferred by users, but that didn't happen. Windows has remained the most popular choice among users.

According to Net Application, a tracking system, in July 2017, among the families of O/S, Windows had about 90 per cent market share, including all kinds of PCs in the world. One of the main reasons of its popularity is the 'ease of operation' — which means any beginner can operate it without much difficulty, with just some basic guidelines. In addition, it also offers advantages like backward integration, better driver support, compatibility with other versions, plug-and-play facility, support for new hardware and usage of a variety of software like photo editors, etc.

Given these advantages since its launch in 1985, it continues to be the most popular O/S for PCs. Starting 1985, MS-DOS, in the new avatar of Windows and with additional feature like GUI, had set on a course that would be unstoppable in computer history. Besides the twenty-six versions for PCs, and others for servers and devices, Windows is today available in 138 languages.

The company's objective all through has been to enhance and enrich the user experience. However, some versions proved to be highly successful, while some not so. Over time, the company has also discontinued support to some versions, while moving on to better alternatives. A closer analysis of this Windows journey would help to understand this progress.

The Many Versions

Despite many different versions introduced over time, many elements in Windows have remained constant. Windows 1 was launched in November 1985, under the supervision of Bill Gates, and ran on the original MS-DOS, heavily relying on a mouse, before it became really popular and an industry-standard. It was the company's first attempt at a GUI, which was to become a PC-fixture later. Because the mouse, as an input device, was a new feature, a game was introduced (Reversi) to help users become familiar with it, whereby they could click on icons using the mouse, rather than the keyboard.

Windows 2 was the next version introduced in 1987. It brought in new features allowing the 'maximizing' and 'minimizing' of windows, and the facility of windows overlapping. It also introduced sophisticated keyboard shortcuts, expanded memory and launched the Control Panel, which has stayed till now. Microsoft Word and Excel too made their appearance for the first time with this version.

Windows 3, launched in 1990, offered improved design, higher memory power and better user-interface — and achieved broad commercial success selling two million copies in the first six months. It also required a hard drive. It was more successful than the earlier versions and challenged Apple's position in the market. It came pre-installed in Zenith computers. With 256 colours and multi-tasking, it made for an enriching user experience.

In 1992, Windows 3.1 came and it brought along True Type fonts, which, in a way, made it a viable publishing platform. The Minesweeper was introduced. It was the first Windows to be distributed on a compact disc (CD-ROM) and would be installed on the hard drive. With a facelift, it also offered a special version, 3.11, Windows for Workgroups, with integrating peer-to-peer networking bundled with it.

Windows 95 (referring to the year 1995) introduced the start button and concept of 'plug and play' to allow gaming, though this was not very successful. It introduced the task bar and for the first time, came embedded with IE. It introduced new features such as support for native 32-bit applications and long file names of up to 255 characters. It was extremely successful, and became practically a fixture on desktops around the world.

The next version in 1998 was built on Windows 95 and brought IE4, Outlook Express, Windows Address Book, Microsoft Chat, and NetShow Player, which was replaced by Media Player 6.2 in its second edition next year. It was a Windows Driver Model with support for USB (short for universal serial bus) composite devices, advanced configuration and power interface, hibernation, multi-monitor configurations and integration with IE4. It also introduced the navigation back-and-forth button and the address bar in Windows Explorer.

Windows ME, the millennium version, was the last Windows version to be based on MS-DOS. It sought to bring a blend between consumer features and the ones being aimed at the enterprise market being offered in Windows 2000. It offered some new concepts to consumers, such as automated system recovery tools, along with IE5.5, Media Player and Windows Movie Maker. As due to some basic flaws it failed to install properly and was buggy, it wasn't well received in the market.

This was followed by Windows 2000 in February 2000, which was the enterprise-twin of the ME version that later formed the basis of Windows XP. It aimed for the business segment, along with the domestic market. Features such as automatic updating and hibernation won it appreciation of the user.

Windows XP has been perhaps the most favoured edition of the Windows line. The company had been trying to enlarge the product's scope by including more enterprise features and it succeeded with Windows XP. Launched in October 2001, it brought both the enterprise mode and the consumer line under one roof. User-friendly elements such as Start Menu and Task

WINDOW(S) TO SUCCESS

Bar got a visual overhaul along with the introduction of other visual effects. Clear Types were introduced to make for easy reading on the liquid crystal display screen and the facility for CD burning was added to the features. With features such as autoplay for CDs, automatic updates and recovery tools, it scored over other editions. It became extremely popular and has had the longest successful run, with three major updates till April 2014, when it gave way for the next one. It was successfully running on 430 million PCs when discontinued.

Security remained an issue with this version as it would get turned off by default, and proved to be a boon for hackers. To counter this complaint, Bill Gates himself supervised the Trustworthy Computing Initiative with a number of elements and updates that would fortify it against attacks. In the market for six years, it was replaced by Windows Vista in January 2007. Despite all the research and innovation that had preceded it, Windows Vista was not able to make its mark in the market. To combat the security threat, the company had perhaps swung to the other extreme. It made the version app-heavy, requiring user account control and user permission to make changes—which was an outcome of Trustworthy Computing. This, in turn, made the operation slow and cumbersome. As many old PCs didn't run on Vista, it didn't quite make the cash register ring. Microsoft was even sued on account of its buggy operation. Media Player II and IE7 debuted on this. However, for gamers it included Media Direct X 10 technology. Anti-spyware, speed recognition, DVD (short for digital versatile disc) Maker and Photo Gallery were some of the new features introduced in this. It was the first Windows to be distributed on DVD. Later, a version with Media Player was created in response to antitrust investigations.

Windows 7 was what Windows Vista should have been. The company's tech team had learnt from some of its mistakes and had come out with a winner. It made its appearance in October 2009. With a less 'dialogue-box overload,' it was crammed with many user-friendly features. It was faster, stable and easier to use. To address possible antitrust issues, it came with a pre-installed IE. A box allowing users to choose between different browsers was also introduced.

As the world had started moving towards touchscreen mode, Microsoft too decided to incorporate some of its elements. Windows 8 was launched in October 2012, and was radically different from the earlier version. It dispensed with the start menu and start button, and brought in touchscreen, with tiled interface icons replacing a list of programmes and icons. Faster than the previous version, it also supported quicker USB 3.0 devices. The Windows Store was introduced, and programmes could still be installed from other iterations of Windows. However, many users feeling more comfortable with the mouse and keyboard features didn't take to it. So, the company went back to the start button and mouse-and-keyboard operation in its Windows 8.1 version.

Windows 10 was released in 2015 and introduced many new features ranging from an updated start menu; Cortana, a virtual assistant for the desktop versions; Action Centre incorporating notifications and quick access to settings; a new web browser, Microsoft Edge; improved multitasking; and updated built-in apps. It has been well-received in the market and is likely to become the reigning Windows version. Beginning in 2015, so far seven major versions of Windows 10 have been released. The company announced that this was Windows's last version, and in future, the O/S would only be supported by updates.

Microsoft Word

From tablets to papyrus in ancient times, to typewriters and word processors in the modern age, humans have continued to look for more convenient and faster ways of written communication. In the late '70s, with advances in microprocessor technology and the emergence of the PC, there were ever newer attempts to produce a smarter and better word processor. With all kinds of scientists and experts making their forays into the field, by the '80s, there were about fifty different types of word processors in the market, offering different features and advantages. The most successful processor around this time was Wordstar, which offered automatic mail merging and controlled 25 per cent of the market.

Against this backdrop, Microsoft entered the market in 1983 with a word processor that ran, not on MS-DOS, but on Xenix. Xenix was a variation of Unix that Microsoft had earlier licenced from AT&T. It was released as a multi-tool Word for Xenix Systems. Over time, different versions were created to suit individual requirements of specific original equipment manufacturers (OEMs). So, between 1983 and 2019, there have been a variety of Word programmes; the major ones include: Versions for IBM (PC) on DOS in 1983, Apple ClassicMac OS in 1985, AT&T Unix PC in 1985, Atari ST in 1988, OS/2 in 1989, MS Windows in 1989, SCO Unix in 1994, and Mac OS (formerly OSX) in 2001. With the growth in other technologies and products, different Word versions were also released for Android in April 2019 and iOS in May 2019.

In all, there have been about sixteen Word versions for Windows, fourteen for classic Macintosh and eight for MS-DOS, besides some others. With a view to upgrade its features and enhance user experience, it has continued to introduce ever new features—ranging from task pane, new XML-based file format, XML data bag, content control, and contextual tabs to file format 'docx', a ribbon-like feature to select page layouts and insert diagrams and images and faster shaping formats.

Modifications were also made to suit the touchscreen PCs and tablet models.

Microsoft Excel

Instead of filling each column and then making calculations at the bottom to reach the final result, one can use a few formulae by clicking a command here and there, and the entire table is filled correctly to the last decimal point—that's the beauty of an electronic spreadsheet, an indispensable tool in accounting today.

Accounting being the basis of economy, humans have been trying for better and smarter ways of bookkeeping since ages. Ever since the worksheet originated after the invention of paper, it had become the mainstay of basic accounting practices. Later, with the development of the computer, attempts were made to create an efficient and faster tool to this effect.

Actually, the word 'spreadsheet' conjures an image of a centrefold or a newspaper with both sides visible—corresponding entries in this case. In this respect, some initial work was done in the early '60s by Richard

Mattessich, business economist and Emeritus Professor at the University of British Columbia. Later, the real breakthrough came with the development of LANPAR (short for LANguage for Programming Arrays at Random) by Rene K. Pardo and Remy Landau in 1970.

Although there was some dispute about patenting, the programme became the de facto system for a variety of calculations and tabulating activities. Soon, it came to be used by leading companies like Bell Canada and AT&T, besides eighteen other local and national telephone companies for their budgeting activities.

However, as work in this direction was going on in different quarters, one may say, the spreadsheet came into its own with the launch of Apple II in 1977. It incorporated a new spreadsheet, VisiCalc (short for Visible Calculator), developed by Bob Frankston and Dan Bricklin of Software Arts. Given the business applications of VisiCalc, it suddenly turned the microcomputer from a gaming device into a serious personal and business tool. It was regarded as a killer application and its sales shot up with a sale of 70,000 copies in the first six years, and over a million in its history. The popularity of Apple II prompted IBM to develop its first PC, and that's how other versions of the spreadsheet came into being.

New competitors that emerged on the scene were SuperCalc, Multiplan and later Lotus 1-2-3. SuperCalc came on the scene in 1981. It was an improvement on VisiCalc and thus got ahead in the market.

A year later, Microsoft introduced its Mutliplan, which was still a step ahead and was targeted towards systems running CP/M (short for Control Program for Microcomputers), MS-DOS, Xenix and many others. As competition was heating up around this time, the appearance of Lotus 1-2-3 changed the entire paradigm. It was developed by Lotus software in 1983, and sought IBM support.

Although IBM had a contractual agreement with the VisiCalc, and it was shipped simultaneously with the IBM-PC, IBM was inclined in its favour because of its obvious advantages. First, the name referred to a three-fold product use: it could be used as a spreadsheet, a graphics package and a database manager. As it got IBM support (like MS-DOS earlier) it was set to sway the market. Another novelty that Lotus introduced was a graph-maker that could make several types of graphs, including pie, bar graphic and line charts.

It began edging out all the other rivals and became the ruling product. Microsoft's Multiplan tried to cope with it but was not so successful. Although it sold over a million copies, it was being outsold, and in the mid-'80s and much of the '90s, Lotus had become the product of choice. In the market, people would ask for the 'Lotus PC'. According to Bill Gates, the main reason for Multiplan's lagging behind was that they had tried to align it with too many ports. In all, there were about a hundred different versions of Multiplan.

But Microsoft, with its competitive spirit, was not going to give up. While it was working on improving its Multiplan, Lotus began to run into rough weather. Microsoft released its improved version of Multiplan as Excel in 1985 for Apple Macintosh, which, for the first time, had a graphical interface. Later, in 1987, Excel 2.0 was released with Windows. During this time, Lotus had begun to suffer some technical issues in converting from a macro assembler to a more portable C language. As Excel was now part of Windows, which was a preferred O/S, its popularity soared. Lotus began to lose ground, and, over time, Excel became the dominant spreadsheet.

So far, over thirteen major versions of Microsoft Excel have been introduced in the market, each offering improved and upgraded features. From the early basic stage, it has gone on to induct features such as toolbars, drawing capabilities, outlining, multi-sheet workbooks, an interface for developers of Visual Basic for Applications, enhanced clipboard, pivot charts, model user forms, sparking graphics, pivot table slicers and single-document interface and charting enhancements.

WINDOW(S) TO SUCCESS

Microsoft PowerPoint

A $14 million acquisition in 1987 has perhaps proved to be a bigger money spinner than most of Microsoft's products or other acquisitions. Initially sceptical about the purchase, Bill Gates's acquisition today is installed on over a billion computers worldwide, and remains one of the most sought-after softwares.

First, some glimpses of business presentation devices and tools. Earlier, a business meeting meant the distribution of certain documents to the members, which would be followed by a discussion, with each member making his notes and speaking in turn. Over time, business houses graduated to chart presentations, and then slide projections when slide projectors came into vogue.

Companies such as Trollman, Genigraphics (a division of GE), Dicomed and others had devised computer workstations on which presentation graphics software could run a large number of slides. But then, it was an expensive and cumbersome process that only large corporations could afford.

In time, with the advent of microcomputers, especially the PCs, the whole game of business presentations underwent a dramatic change. So, in the early '80s, a large number of companies had begun to develop presentation software, and in 1987, Microsoft too had initiated its own project to this effect. But then, to speed up the project, the company started toying with the idea of an acquisition.

Out of the two options, Jeff Raikes of Microsoft preferred Presenter of Forethought because of its clear advantage of overhead presentations. Initially, Gates was a little unsure about the acquisition and had thought that the presentation application could be a feature of Word, and not a separate product in itself. In time, he got convinced otherwise and Forethought was acquired by Microsoft in July 1987.

To go back in time, Forethought had earlier initiated a project in 1984 with an aim to develop a presentation application for Apple Macintosh and Microsoft Windows. The work progressed satisfactorily and they were able to produce a major design specification document for Apple. On the positive outcome of this, Forethought was assured funding by Apple in January 1987. Later, in April 1987, Forethought was ready with PowerPoint 1.0 for Macintosh, and the first product run was of 10,000 units, which got lapped up by the market. Later, in July, the company was acquired by Microsoft. All through, the product was called 'Presenter', but was later named 'PowerPoint,' as the name 'Presenter' had already been registered by someone else. Robert Gaskins, one of the two lead developers, called it 'PowerPoint' as it assured certain power to the individual presenter.

WINDOW(S) TO SUCCESS

In mid-1988, a new version, PowerPoint 2.0, was released for Apple that went colour (from the earlier black and white) with thirty-five slides. Although initially received well in the market, PowerPoint was not able to acquire a desired share in view of many competing entities. One major reason for this was that as yet, the PowerPoint version for Windows had not been released and most of the PCs in the market ran on MS-DOS, which used the presentation software of Harvard Graphics and Lotus Freelance Plus.

It was only when the first version of PowerPoint 2.0 for Windows was marketed that the scene began to change. It was able to ride the popularity wave of Windows like many other products, took lead over Apple and never looked back. Since then, its worldwide market share has been estimated at 95 per cent.

Today, PowerPoint is available in 102 languages, including Arabic, Assamese, Bulgarian, Polish, Punjabi and Turkish. Compatible versions for Android and iOS have also been released.

THE NEXT CHAPTER IN TECH

*I really had a lot of dreams when I was a kid,
and I think a great deal of that grew out of the fact
that I had a chance to read a lot.*
— BILL GATES

Microsoft and New Technologies

In order to reduce its dependence on the Windows and Office products, Microsoft had begun to divert resources towards many other areas since the beginning. In some areas it found success while in some others, it was not able to make much headway. However, two segments where the company has performed impressively in recent times are cloud computing and AI. Let's have a closer look at the developments in these areas.

THE NEXT CHAPTER IN TECH

Azure Cloud Computing

First of all, what's cloud computing? In the beginning of the Internet, a lot of people would remark that 80 per cent use of the facility was for email. In time, it dawned on people that when you could send letters and pictures through email, why not big files and data? And thus was born the idea of cloud computing, which began to take concrete shape with Amazon releasing Elastic Compute Cloud in 2006. As the idea caught on, Microsoft saw in it a big opportunity and released Microsoft Azure in February 2010.

In fact, the facility offers a range of advantages to business houses. Before the Internet, they needed to have dedicated servers to store data and files. Now with the Cloud, any company can buy server-space in the network at a much reduced cost. So, no need of capital investment on server and maintenance and hiring of staff. The facility is not just limited to data storage or retrieval but a host of other technologies that individual companies wouldn't have been able to access earlier. As the service gives value, it's been catching on.

Today, Microsoft Azure offers a host of advantages to companies ranging from functions for server-less computing, virtual machine scale sets, service fabric for microservices and container orchestration, virtual network and content delivery network to traffic manager, file and disk storage, Azure-developed test labs, site recovery, container registry, SQL (Structured Query Language)-based databases and related tools, stream analytics, tools for developing artificial capabilities, a variety of machine learning, security centre, visual studio team services, resource manager, log analytics, automation and more.

Given its plus points, it today stands as one of the top vendors (and contenders) in the field, having earned a reputation as a 'highly reliable and secure public Cloud provider.' One of the main reasons for its surging ahead is the fact that a large number of networks round the globe are Windows-backed. And since Azure offers virtually seamless connectivity, it's a service of choice. Above all, it offers a vibrant ecosystem by having collaborative arrangements with many other computer companies like Red Hat, Hewlett Packard, Adobe, Cisco and others.

Microsoft has been deliberately targeting government institutions, 'highlighting its security and compliance capabilities,' and its website claims that Azure has been recognized 'as the most trusted Cloud for US government institutions, including a FedRAMP high authorization that covers 118 Azure services.'

With Microsoft playing an aggressive player in the arena, Cloud wars seem to be hotting up. No wonder, Azure has begun to play catch up with the pioneer, Amazon Web Services. In an October 2018 report, it was stated that for the first time, Azure had beaten Amazon Web Services in revenue, recording $26.7 billion to Amazon's $23.4 billion in the past twelve months. With these rivals in neck-to-neck competition, IBM, also an early entrant, is today lagging behind. To counter this, IBM acquired Red Hat for $34 billion in October 2018, an acquisition that added $3 billion to the company's revenue annually.

Satya Nadella, CEO, Microsoft, made the company's policy clear in this regard recently, 'Our Cloud platform and tools enable our customers to build tech intensity while ensuring we're addressing their tough questions around trust—both trust in technology and trust that they have a partner whose business model is aligned to their success.'

Clearly, Azure Cloud Computing seems to have a great future ahead, as it hopes to provide another security-net layer to the company like Windows has over time.

Artificial Intelligence

In the 18th-19th centuries, people would tie giant wings to their arms and try to fly from heights. Just as flying has always caught people's fancy, the idea of a machine-man has been equally fascinating—a walking, talking robot that would do your bidding. They say, writers imagine today and scientists confirm tomorrow. Writers, artists and film-makers have let their imagination fly in this direction since long. We have mention of Talos, a giant machine man in Greek mythology. The idea had continued to excite many a modern writer. Mary Shelley, a 19th-century writer, had come out with the story of a creature, Frankenstein, who, once created with the help of machines, goes out of human control and becomes a monster. In recent times, feature films using elements of AI, like *Star Trek; RoboCop; I, Robot; The Terminator* and *The Matrix* have been big box office draws.

While on one hand, scientists and researchers have continued to demonstrate the potential in the field, on the other, many people have also expressed their concerns about progress in AI. Stephen Hawking, the renowned scientist and astronomer, was quite apprehensive about the technology and had once said, 'The development of full artificial intelligence could spell the end of the human race...It [AI] would take off on its own, and re-design itself at an ever-increasing rate. Humans, who are limited by slow biological evolution, couldn't compete and would be superseded.'

But then, AI is one of the frontline sciences today, with large investments being made into it. We have factories in advanced countries where a large quantum of work is handled by robots. Robotics is also a discipline in universities and engineering institutes.

In retrospect, concrete progress in this direction was only made possible with the development of computers. Scientists began to think that if a computer can perform increasingly complex functions, why can it not develop independent thinking? And thus was born the concept of AI. Work on it had begun in right earnest at Dartmouth College, New Hampshire, US, in 1956. Scientists and engineers from some of the leading facilities such as Massachusetts Institute of Technology (MIT), Carnegie Mellon University (CMU) and IBM had begun working on such projects, and in a few years were able to report significant progress. Observers and the press called some of their achievements 'astonishing'. It was found that the computer could beat humans in standard tasks like solving certain mathematical problems and applying theorems, etc. They were even found to be playing board games like Checkers better than their human counterparts.

Encouraged by the success of these breakthroughs, the US Department of Defense, forever looking to beat the enemy, increased their funding and laboratories were set up all over the world. Herbert Alexander Simon, a leading economist and cognitive scientist, declared around that time, 'Machines will be capable, within twenty years, of doing any work a man can do.' Another leading authority in AI, Marvin Minsky agreed with him and said, 'Within a generation... the problem of creating Artificial Intelligence will substantially be solved.' However, the confidence these proponents of the discipline exuded at that time gradually began to wane as unexpected problems and hurdles were encountered. The government cut down on grants, and a long AI winter set in.

Research in this area was again revived in the '80s with the success of the expert system (a machine that emulates the human decision-making process), and with the launch of the Japanese fifth-generation computer. Although the AI market had reached over a billion dollars in 1985, some setbacks again slowed progress in this area. After the late '90s, a major push came in this area with the development of more powerful computers and advances in other fields. Today, we have robot-driven manufacturing facilities round the globe and intelligent machines in households like Siri, Alexa and Google Home.

What's Artificial Intelligence?

AI is the infusion of human characteristics into a machine. To take a common example, when we moved from the grinding stone to the electricity-operated mixer-grinder, it was a movement from manual to automatic. With one control, we can make a machine work day in and day out. With advancement in technology, man was looking at moving from automatic auto-rotation to a machine that, with minimal human supervision, would be able to take independent decisions and complete a task without mistakes.

So, just as we use our intelligence to do certain tasks, the machine too uses its 'artificial intelligence' to perform certain duties. Though both have limitations, machine intelligence has more of it. To understand the issue, it's important to see how the concept of AI has developed over time, how it is created and how it's becoming increasingly useful for humankind.

We know that, at the root, all computer calculations and performances are algorithms, which in other words, are a set of instructions to the computer, in a pre-set, rigid, coded format. In simple terms, the computer is told (by algorithms) that $2 + 2 = 4$, and so, when asked a question to this effect, it gives the correct reply. Now, if a computer is allowed to modify its algorithms on its own, and is set free from the rigid format, make its own deductions and derivations through relative correlations, it enters the realm of AI. It might even offer you advice and guide your decisions. It's this switching from the pre-set mode to 'independent-decision mode' that infuses AI characteristics in a computer.

Now, for instance, the intelligent machine (Google Home, Siri or Alexa) knows that clouds are formed by water vapours and bring rain, and if you're going out, it might advise you to 'take an umbrella or raincoat'. It has derived this conclusion on its own from a set of pre-existing algorithms fed into it. Or for that matter, the machine knows that you're a man of means, and also another set of information that 'gentlemen prefer blondes'; based on this, it might advise you against dating a 'redhead'. What the machine is doing is it's making its own derivations and deductions based on pre-existing information in its processing system.

Microsoft and AI

As is customary with Microsoft, it has always kept up with trends in the market. It had begun to make investments in AI early, and as time passed, continued to show deeper interest in it. One of its first major projects in this field was Kinetic, which used motion-sensing inputs to help users control and interact with the gaming console. The player would just use gestures and spoken commands with the webcam as an accessory to aid in operation, and without going for the gaming controller, to play the game. Initially, it was developed for Microsoft's video-gaming consoles, XboxOne and Xbox360.

Although gaming consoles continue to be extremely popular with users, somehow the Kinetic inputs didn't find much traction with players. But one positive fallout of this research has been that because of its low-cost advanced features, it has found application in many other fields, including the company's cloud computing platform Azure. Another major development in this field has been the use of simultaneous language-translations on Skype. Skype, which had facilitated communication over the Internet, had been acquired by Microsoft in 2010. Now with its AI add-ons, the simultaneous translation in many languages, including English, French, German, Chinese, Italian, Spanish and others, is available.

Although AI on its own may not be producing perceptible revenue to impact the company's books, its indirect role is being felt in every area of operation to improve its performance and productivity. It's making inroads in every field of human activity, whether easy or difficult, simple or complex. Aware of its growing importance, Microsoft set up its Artificial Intelligence and Research Group in 2016 with 5,000 computer scientists and engineers. The group has been making AI contributions in different areas, ranging from language translators, gaming consoles, improving machine learning, examining the societal and individual impact of the spread of intelligent technologies and developing interactive tools (like Word Writer, etc.), innovative platforms for cyber-physical systems and robotics.

THE STUMBLING BLOCKS

To win big, you sometimes have to take big risks.
— BILL GATES

Flip Side of Growth

Growth has its downside too — on one hand, it makes you go with the flow to keep up with the momentum and sometimes even overstep the bounds of law; and on the other, your product's popularity can tempt others to produce duplicates and make you suffer revenue loss. In both cases, damage control is necessary to safeguard one's long-term interests. Bill Gates, in his journey through Microsoft, has experienced both kinds of scenarios — let's see how he coped with them.

Antitrust Case

The government's position in a free-market economy is that everyone has the complete liberty to grow, to maximize his potential — but no freedom can be unbridled. It's the government's duty to ensure a level-playing field for all. If with money or tech power, an entity tries to curb others' right to grow, or abuses its dominant status in any other way, it needs to be checked. This is the basis of the Sherman Antitrust Act, which was enacted by the US Government in 1890 to 'protect trade and commerce against unlawful restraints and monopolies.' The objective was to ensure a level-playing field and fair play for all — and the case against Microsoft was essentially seeking to uphold the spirit of this law.

Against this background, sometime in the early '90s, it came to the notice of authorities that because of its dominant position in the PC O/S market, Microsoft had been misusing its power in pressurizing its OEM customers into coercive deals. In 1992, the Federal Trade Commission began an independent inquiry to check if Microsoft was abusing its monopoly position over the PC O/S market.

As nothing substantive could be established, the inquiry resulted in a deadlock, with two commissioners on both sides voting for and against the move, and the inquiry was closed in 1993. However, in the same year, on 21 May, then US Attorney General Janet Reno took a suo moto cognizance of the case and began an inquiry on her own. In her inquiry, she found lapses and overstepping of the bounds of law by Microsoft. She also discovered that owing to its strong product in Windows O/S, the company had been subjecting customers to a variety of unfair deals.

On 27 July 1994, the US Department of Justice (DoJ) put on record its findings, stating that between 1988 and 1994, Microsoft had abused its monopoly position in the PC software market by inducing many OEMs to pay a royalty for each computer it sold containing a particular microprocessor, irrespective of whether the computer sold was with Microsoft O/S or with some other O/S. For example, if a company sold one hundred computers but installed Windows on only sixty, it still had to pay a licence fee for hundred. This would naturally discourage PC manufacturers from using other O/Ss. In other words, it was a way to penalize the manufacturer for using a different product from Windows O/S.

As there was some other evidence too of wrongdoing on Microsoft's part, the DoJ made Microsoft adhere to certain conditions, whereby the company agreed not to tie other products with the sale of Windows. It was, however, free to incorporate them as additional features in the same software, if necessary. Among some others, it also put restrictions on the company to have more than a certain period of contract for sale.

However, the real problem for Microsoft was to begin later. It was after the arrival of the Internet that Microsoft was in for a major face-off with the government. In the beginning of the '90s, the IT industry was poised for a big change with the arrival of the Internet. It had introduced many new elements in the market that were to result in a major transformation of the industry and the general market on the whole. As the idea had begun to catch up, more and more servers were being linked and a large number of files and data were being uploaded to the Net.

Someone had remarked in the beginning of the Internet that it 'is the biggest library in the world, but all the books are on the floor.' So, along with the growth of the Internet, there was also an immediate need for an efficient browser that would help users access data available on the Net. So, there ensued a 'browser war' with different manufacturers competing to produce a better browser.

Browser War

The first major browser to hit the market was the NCSA (short for National Centre for Supercomputing Applications) Mosaic, which was released in September

1993. A graphical browser that was later ported to Apple Macintosh and Windows, it displayed images in line with the document's texts. It fired people's imagination and triggered a great interest in the Internet. Marc Andreessen, who was the leader for Mosaic, later quit NCSA and formed his own company, Netscape Communications Corporation. It released its flagship browser in October 1994, which was to take the market by storm, and create serious issues with Microsoft. It was one of the main reasons for the antitrust suit brought against the company.

Microsoft, which hadn't entered the fray yet, came out with its own browser, IE, in August 1995. Next year in 1996, while Netscape's share was 86 per cent, that of IE was only 10 per cent. To increase its share, Microsoft adopted its typical strategy to piggyback its browser on Windows. It began to bundle the IE with Windows, which meant it came free to Windows users. Since Windows was practically on every second PC, IE began to increase its market share exponentially. On the other hand, Netscape was a fine product, but unlike IE, had to be bought separately and took time to download, which was rather cumbersome. So, within four years of release, IE's share had reached 75 per cent, and by 1999, it had gone up to 99 per cent.

In view of these developments, an antitrust suit was brought against Microsoft by the DoJ and the Attorney

Generals of twenty US states for using monopoly practices to illegally thwart competition by using its software dominance. The case began on 18 May 1998. It was argued that the company had forced PC makers to install IE along with its Windows system. The DoJ was represented by David Boies. The case, which lasted about one and a half years, saw Bill Gates's various testimonies and bitter arguments from both sides. A witness quoted a senior Microsoft employee as admitting to the company's intention to 'extinguish' and 'smother' rival Netscape and to 'cut off Netscape's air supply'.

In support of its claims, Microsoft presented many videotapes, but many of them were later found to be doctored. Gates was called 'evasive and nonresponsive' by a source present in the court. He argued over the definitions of words like 'compete', 'concern', 'ask' and 'we'. He repeated the expression, 'I don't recall,' so many times that it even made the judge chuckle. Microsoft argued that by such practices, the government was simply trying to prevent innovation and thwart the development of new products, under pressure from 'jealous' and incompetent companies.

On the whole, Microsoft was on a weak wicket, and the judge, Thomas Penfield Jackson, ruled against them (in two parts): On 3 April 2000, he indicted the company; and in June 2000, ordered a breakup of

Microsoft as a 'remedy'. He ordered that the company be split into two parts: one to produce and manage the O/S and the other for software products. Microsoft appealed against the decision, and the Court of Appeals for the District of Columbia Circuit overturned Judge Jackson's ruling against Microsoft, and later, on 6 September 2001, the DoJ announced that it was not seeking the breakup of the company and would rather seek a lesser antitrust penalty. Microsoft agreed to settlements with PC manufacturers, with the assurance that a lot of their concerns would be addressed through different concessions.

During this time, an open letter was addressed to President Clinton by 240 leading economists, whereby they said that through many provisions of the Antitrust Act, the government was thwarting innovation and progress, and should avoid playing in the hands of inept companies. On the other side of the divide, critics of 'monopolistic practices' have continued to argue that companies such as Microsoft, which have become behemoths, would remain difficult to control much to the detriment of general welfare.

Anti-piracy

Piracy has always been a concern for Microsoft. Bill Gates got a taste of it rather early, when he

THE STUMBLING BLOCKS

had designed the first major programme for Altair. Although the product had become quite popular with computer enthusiasts, its popularity also proved to be a bane. Gates discovered that a pre-market copy had leaked into the community and was being copied and circulated in large numbers.

Gates had always held that talent and creativity could never flourish without the desired support and incentive. In February 1976, he wrote an open letter to hobbyists in MITS's in-house newsletter, in which he said, 'More than 90 per cent of users of MS Altair Basic had not paid Microsoft...And by doing so, Altair hobby market was in the danger of eliminating incentive for any professional developers to produce, distribute and market high-quality software.'

In fact, piracy is the bane of any maker of a product that can be easily duplicated—music, video, film, book and now software. For the creator, it's a double whammy—loss of revenue, and a dampener for the talent, thus restricting future flowering of ideas. However, in the context of Microsoft, we need to take a broader and historical view of the problem.

Although Gates had got a taste of it earlier, but after the popularity of his MS-DOS and, later, Windows, he was to face the real dimension of the problem. With the PC offering a whole range of advantages, its demand had begun to rise not only in the US and the West, but also the rest of the world. Since Windows was the O/S of choice, its growth too registered a steady increase.

It was the early days in 1993, when a trade journal in the US had reported that while the 'US has lost edge in the global manufacturing industry, it had gained in the computer software business.' Around this time, the US had over 80 per cent market share of computer software in the world. But then, the journal also pointed towards an accompanying problem. According to general estimates, the US was losing about $2 billion annually on account of software piracy in the country alone—and five times in the rest of the world.

It was 1993 when the world PC market was at a nascent stage. Over time, the problem could still be handled in the US and the West through better surveillance methods and law enforcement, but was to become more acute in the coming time elsewhere. With the growth in the Chinese, Indian, South American and other markets of the world, it was set to assume alarming proportions.

Interestingly, in 2004, during a visit to China, Bill Gates was asked by a senior government official about Microsoft's income from China. When he mentioned a figure, the official was surprised and he asked the interpreter to double-check with Gates. In his view, the figure was too low. But it was correct. In China, the problem of software piracy was rampant, and it was estimated that about 90 per cent PCs ran on pirated software.

In November 2018, Steve Ballmer told Fox News that in China alone, Microsoft was losing to the tune of $10 billion due to piracy. The problem has been no better in India, another major market for PCs. At current prices, when pirated Windows software is available for ₹130, the original software costs around ₹9,000. The reality check is, while large corporations, on account of visibility and transparency, cannot afford to risk pirated software, individuals and small businesses escape the radar of surveillance and save on the expensive programme. In fact, in India, very often the hardware vendor himself would offer a free Windows copy along with the computer to boost his sale and retain the competitive edge. Why would the computer dealer lose his business? And who would peep into your house to see what kind of software you're using?

In view of the increasing problem, Microsoft has continued to deal with the issue in a variety of ways—ranging from online checks and offer of incentives and cost-cutting, to physical action with support of local law enforcement agencies. In 2009, the company launched its Windows Genuine Advantage, whereby it informed the user about the benefits of using genuine software, and outlined how it would provide better security and performance with regular updates. Despite the growth in the problem, it had become possible for the Microsoft team to detect the counterfeit software by detecting the IP address. In this case, the PC's background screen would go black and a message at the bottom would warn, 'You could be a victim of counterfeit software'. The user was urged to procure genuine software and get the benefits.

The company was supported by a lot of countries in its drive against the menace. In 2000, it was able to take legal action against piracy and illegal counterfeiting in twenty-two countries with the help of local authorities. In many countries like Argentina, Brazil, Canada, Colombia, Germany, Hong Kong, Peru, Poland, Philippines, China, Romania, the US and the UK, operations were carried to address the problem. It was reported in 2001, that over five million units of illegal software and hardware products of Microsoft were seized worldwide in the previous year.

In 2009, Mexican authorities conducted a massive raid with about 300 guards on an illegal operation in Los Reyes, a town in Mexico. In the operation, three people were arrested who had been duplicating Microsoft CDs, MS Office software and Xbox video games. Over fifty duplicating machines were also seized. In India again, there have been a number of raids by authorities in offices of some companies suspected of using counterfeit products.

THE STUMBLING BLOCKS

In relation to the Chinese market, Microsoft adopted some specific measures. It drastically cut Windows's price to deter users from going for the pirated stuff. Lenovo is China's largest PC manufacturer, with 36.7 per cent market share. It used to ship bare computers, sans O/S. In 2013, Microsoft was able to persuade the company to sell hardware with pre-installed software.

The Linux Alternative

Some industry commentators have remarked that Microsoft is not too serious about combating the piracy problem as it has its own contribution in making Bill Gates the richest person in the world. They say that the easy and 'almost free' availability of Windows software made a whole new generation part of the Windows ecosystem, who, when they later became part of the workforce, preferred Windows systems at offices, and thus gave a further fillip to Windows use and helped to spur demand.

Looking back, since the mid-'90s, one of the main contenders to Windows has been Linux. Linux is an open-source software and, thus, free. As against Windows, it can be downloaded by any user, who could make his own alterations and modifications and use it. However, it's rather cumbersome to use and involves a greater degree of effort on the user's part. It has been more suitable for server applications. The main and distinct advantage of Windows has been its user-friendly features, making it extremely easy to use, even for a beginner with no previous computer experience. So, it was contented that while pirated Windows had been easily available and almost free, why would a common user opt for Linux? Had people shifted to Linux on account of the cost factor, Windows wouldn't have become the phenomenon it's today — and Microsoft wouldn't be so big. Thus, in a way, the Windows piracy has had a certain positive fallout for the company.

'TO WHOM MUCH IS GIVEN, MUCH IS EXPECTED'

We have to find a way to make the aspects of capitalism that serve wealthier people serve poorer people as well.
—BILL GATES

Bill and Melinda Gates Foundation

If Bill Gates got his competitive spirit from his Protestant upbringing, he got his altruistic nature from his mother. Mary Maxwell Gates was a lifelong community activist and also served on the Board of UWC. It was her firm belief that every individual must have some room in his life and heart for others—and especially, if you're blessed. 'To whom much is given (from him) much is expected'—this teaching was part of the Christian values inculcated among children at a young age. '(Mary) never stopped pressing me to do more for others,' Gates said in his Harvard commencement speech in 2007.

In 1991, his mother forced him to drive down from his vacation home to meet Warren Buffet. As Gates didn't think much of him, he was reluctant to meet him. 'Look, he just buys and sells pieces of paper,' said Gates. 'That's not real value-added. I don't think we'd have much in common.' But his meeting with Buffet proved to be the beginning of a lifelong association for both, and earned Bill another comrade-in-arms for a common cause.

Bill's mother was fortunate to see her son's wealth grow tremendously before her death from breast cancer in 1994. At that time, Gates was listed as one of the richest men in the world. His setting up of the foundation was, in a way, a personal tribute to his mother's memory.

In 1994, Gates had started the William H. Gates Foundation. Later, he and his wife combined three family foundations in 2000, and renamed them as Bill and Melinda Gates Foundation, to which Bill donated stock worth $5 billion. Its co-chair have been Bill Gates, Melinda Gates and William H. Gates Sr., with Susan Desmond-Hellman as the CEO. Today, it's the largest private endowment fund in the world with a holding of $50.7 billion.

'TO WHOM MUCH IS GIVEN, MUCH IS EXPECTED'

The basic objectives behind the foundation are: One, address healthcare issues in the world and reduce extreme poverty; and two, in the US, expand educational opportunities and improve access to IT.

During its twenty-year journey, it has traversed a long distance, achieving many a landmark through its fruitful endeavours. As on April 2014, the foundation came to be organized under five key functions:

- Global Development Division
- Global Health Division
- United States Division
- Global Policy and Advocacy Division
- Global Growth and Opportunity Division

In June 2006, Warren Buffet, the owner of Berkshire Hathaway and then the richest man in the world with a net worth of $64 billion sought involvement in the Foundation and pledged to contribute on an annual basis a certain amount, with an offering of $1.5 billion in the first year.

Since its inception, the organization has been able to meet success on the various goals it had set out to achieve. One unique feature about the Foundation is its accent on transparency, conspicuously absent in many other charities of the kind. It allows the benefactors to access information in respect to the areas where their money is being spent.

The projects for which grants have been made since the beginning are:

- $20 million to Carnegie Mellon University (CMU) for a new building to be named as Gates Centre for Computer Science, which opened in 2009.
- Supporting the International Rice Research Institute (IRRI).
- $20 million to MIT for the construction of a computer laboratory building called William H. Gates Building.
- $6 million for the construction of the Gates Computer Science Building at Stanford University completed in 1996.
- Establishing the Cambridge Scholarship with an endowment of $210 million at Cambridge University, on the lines of the Rhodes Scholarship, for students across the world.
- $146 million to the Alliance for a Green Revolution in Africa (AGRA).
- $777 million to The Global Fund to Fight AIDS, Tuberculosis and Malaria.
- $334 million for medicines for the Malaria Venture.
- $166 million for the World Health Organization's

Nigeria country office.
- $199.5 million for the Clinton Health Access Initiative.
- $338.4 million for the Global Alliance for TB Drug Development.
- $5 million to the International Justice Mission (IJM).

So far, broadly, the foundation has worked in four areas: Health, financial services for the poor, sanitation, and agricultural development.

It has been able to make much headway with activities focusing mainly on areas that have included financially helping IJM combat sex trafficking and slavery. It was particularly successful in Project Lantern in the city of Cebu in Philippines.

In the area of education, the creation of Gates's Cambridge Scholarships has helped students from all over the world in pursuing higher studies. Financial inclusion endeavours have helped marginalized sections living below $2 a day to create savings accounts, seek insurance and other financial services. The foundation has also made grants to conduct field surveys in the area of microfinance, which includes covering Pro Mujer, a microfinance network in Latin America, and Grameen Foundation, a US-based non-governmental organization working on similar lines in the developing world.

Through its Agricultural Development Division, the foundation has been able to cover IRRI (headquartered in Philippines) for rice research to develop a better variant of rice to address the issue of Vitamin A deficiency. It has also been assisting AGRA, in partnership with the Rockefeller Foundation, to give a boost to agricultural productivity with research in Africa—with the Gates Foundation contributing $100 million and the Rockefeller Foundation $50 million.

Through its Water, Sanitation and Hygiene programme, or WASH, the foundation has launched a variety of projects for sanitation and hygiene improvement. Today, around one billion people in the world have no sanitation facility, numbering about 600 million in India alone. Since about 2011, the Foundation has been funding various projects in India to end the practice of open defecation. Given the specific and unique problems in individual countries, the programme has been focusing on developing innovative sanitation techniques for slum dwellers in sub-Saharan Africa and South Asian countries. Here, the challenge has been to develop systems that are independent of piped water and sewage facilities.

The Reinvent the Toilet Challenge programme launched by the Foundation has been focusing on developing on-site and off-site water-treatment solutions, and to create a toilet that not only removes pathogens from excreta, but also recovers resources such as energy, clean water and nutrients. The Omni Processor has been another combustion-based system that converts faecal sludge into energy and drinking water.

Unlike in the West, where lifestyle-related diseases are more common, African and Asian counties have been struggling to deal with issues like AIDS, malaria and tuberculosis (TB). The Foundation's Health Division has donated to programmes for the improvement of nutrition and agriculture in Africa, and for polio eradication, vaccines (including for children and against TB) and immunization, HIV/AIDS patients, a cheaper high-tech TB test and a next-generation condom for planned parenthood through a variety of projects.

Under its education initiatives, it has created scholarships at prestigious universities for bright students from all over the world. Cambridge, Cornell, Harvard and many others are sought-after institutions among scholars for seeking excellence in education. By facilitating students' entry into these institutions, it has served the larger cause of education. Besides scholarships for individual students, the Foundation has also been making grants for libraries and other projects.

However, despite a lot of good work and well-meaning initiatives, the Foundation has often come under criticism from different social organizations and sections of media. It has been alleged that the charity favours its preferred companies and many of its programmes in the ultimate analysis go to benefit Microsoft, such as promotion of IT education in the US.

That aside, the Foundation has continued to earn laurels for outstanding work in poverty alleviation and assistance in the eradication of many infectious diseases. In 2005, Bill and Melinda Gates, along with musician Bono, were named Persons of the Year by *Time* magazine for their outstanding charitable work. In 2013, Hillary Clinton launched a partnership between the Bill and Melinda Gates Foundation and the Clinton Foundation for the gathering and study of data on women around the world. In 2007, the foundation was presented with the Indira Gandhi Peace Award by the then President of India, Pratibha Singh Patil, and in 2015, Bill and Melinda Gates jointly received India's third highest civil honour, Padma Bhushan. In 2016, then President of the US, Barack Obama conferred on Bill and Melinda Gates the Presidential Medal for Freedom for their philanthropic work.

THE OTHER FOUNDER

Money has no utility to me beyond a point.
— BILL GATES

Bill and Paul

The relationship of Bill and Paul has few parallels in the business world, and given the difference in their personalities, it's not too surprising that it didn't last a lifetime. The two had their good moments and bad moments, but in the long run, it didn't last as ideally it should have. As the contours of their relationship and the subtle layering of their interactions is so central to our subject, we need to go deeper into it.

In teenage, usually children have a group of friends and can be seen playing around in a park or home, and having fun together. However, Bill's life had taken an unusual turn after forging a friendship with Paul, two years his senior at school. Computers being new in those days, they were quite fascinated by the machine; and they were good at math, so they took to it quite naturally. During school time, they would be busy in the computer room in school, and in the late hours, land up at the Computer Science Library of the University of Washington nearby, to hone their programming skills. As Paul was older and fond of reading, his horizon was much wider than Gates's. Bill, in a way, felt a little grateful to him for keeping him alongside. 'Guys those days usually didn't hang out with kids two years their junior,' Bill had remarked, talking of Paul.

However, as we've talked in detail about their professional collaboration and business together, here our focus is mainly on their personal relationship. There's no doubt that personality-wise they were very different people. And as they began to grow, the differences kind of got accentuated. Bill admits, that though being far ahead of his times, Paul was not happy being a manager and confined to a desk. He had many diverse interests and he sought a much larger broader life; the outdoors excited him.

On the other hand, Bill, happy to give himself to computers and wishing to build a great company, would often end up working late at night at the office. 'Bill would say, "I wonder what it's like to run a Fortune 500 company",' recalls Paul. 'And I'd say,

THE OTHER FOUNDER

"I don't know."' As there was pressure to build the company and keep up with the competition, the two would often have arguments over work-related issues. 'Bill has a very intense discussion style,' says Paul. 'My style is very much more logical.'

While talking to Paul, after the publication of his book *Idea Man: A Memoir by the Co-founder of Microsoft*, interviewer Lesley Stahl in CBS's *60 Minutes*, described it as a very 'bitter book', referring to the difficult relationship Bill and Paul shared. Paul commented on Gates's aggressive approach, which could at times be 'browbeating, leading to personal verbal attacks.' He recalls incidents when the two would land up having 'screaming matches,' which would go on for hours. 'It's really exhausting,' he says. 'I was too angry and proud to tell Bill point blank that "sometimes working with you is like being in hell."' He remembers how Bill would always be pushing him to work more—even more than he would others.

In the initial stages, there was also the question of cash flow. 'I was concerned about having enough money in the bank to pay the next month's salaries,' says Bill. And Bill thought as if the responsibility of running the company was entirely on his shoulders. As time passed, Bill had started developing a feeling that he had been sharing a greater burden of the work. The relationship was on a downslide, and the precipitating moment came after Paul was diagnosed with Hodgkin's lymphoma in 1982.

Bill and Paul Part Ways

'As I was passing by Bill's office one night, I heard Bill and Steve Ballmer talking about me,' said Paul in his interview to Stahl. 'They were basically talking about diluting my share almost to nothing.' For him, it was a very 'shocking and disheartening moment': 'I was perhaps in the middle of my radiation therapy.' He says he confronted them about their plan to rip him off. Bill perhaps felt a little embarrassed by his behaviour and wished to make amends later. 'Later that night, Bill sent Steve to my house to apologize,' said Paul.

'He sent Steve?' quipped the interviewer. 'Bill didn't come himself?'

'No, he sent Steve,' said Paul.

As Paul decided to leave, there came up the contentious issue of ownership. Both being 50 per cent partners, Paul rightfully thought of himself as half-owner of the company. It's said that Gates asked him to give him part of his shares as Bill 'had done almost everything on BASIC'. On the one hand, the two knew that in the O/S development, Paul had had a larger contribution. However, Allen agreed to split the shares

60:40 in Bill's favour. Gates later negotiated the deal to a 64:36 split. The company had been doing well, and Bill had great plans for the future and felt quite confident of high growth. Against this backdrop, Bill was tempted to increase his holding, and in 1983 again tried to buy out Allen at $5 per share, but Allen refused and left the company, practically one-third owner of Microsoft.

Allen may not be as smart a businessman as Bill was, but given his tech knowledge and having known Bill and Microsoft, could clearly see where the company was going. Holding on to his Microsoft shares was perhaps the smartest thing he did in his life, which proved to be, for him, the biggest fortune of all. When Microsoft went public on 13 March 1986, with an initial public offering (IPO) of $21 per share (by the end of the day, the share value had risen to $35.50), it made Paul's investment six times what Bill was offering him at the time of separation. In 1983, when he left Microsoft, Paul could virtually see skies opening up for him. The treatment had worked and he had been completely cured of the disease. He was very rich and free to pursue his dreams.

Paul after Microsoft

First, a look at Paul's family and background. Paul was born on 21 January 1953 in Seattle, Washington, in a middle-class family. He had a younger sister, Jody Allen. Both his parents, father Kenneth Sam Allen and mother Edna Faye Allen, were librarians, his father being an associate director of Washington University libraries. Being academically inclined themselves, they were keen to see Paul do well at school and thus paid extra attention to his curriculum and studies. Paul was fond of reading and his mother would get him a variety of junior science fiction and other books to keep his interest alive. Given all these factors, he turned out to be a bright student, passing out of Lakeside with a perfect 1600 (out of 1600) in his SAT result.

We're already quite familiar about his early school and professional life leading to the setting up of Microsoft. What concerns us here is what followed after his leaving Microsoft and how he tried to make the best of his resources in following his dreams.

After being diagnosed with lymphoma, he was fortunate that the gloom didn't last long. He was able to beat the disease with radiation therapy and was declared cancer-free after a few months of treatment. Being one-third owner of Microsoft, he was now very rich. Just thirty-one and healthy again, he saw the world opening before him. He wished to pursue his dreams like never before. 'I didn't have any regrets of leaving,' he said.

In the words of Bill Gates, Paul was 'immensely

curious' and had very wide-ranging interests: 'He read more science fiction than I ever did... His office would be full of all kinds of magazines, though a little messy, represented his wide interests. He always wanted to find new and different things, always a little ahead of his time.'

So, unlike Bill, who was happy to pursue his computer goals, Paul had diverse interests, ranging from arts to music, sports to travel, and entertainment to philanthropy. He was on the threshold of realizing most of his dreams. In 1986, he set up Vulcan Inc. along with his sister, Jody — a company through which his assets and investments would be managed.

Given his wealth, he was able to lay a roadmap for his future life. While on one hand, he made investments in fields that interested him, on the other, he also used his money for philanthropic purposes and research in science and technology projects. His investments ranged from cable and film entertainment to real estate and sports. *The Wall Street Journal* called Allen's South Lake Union real estate investment as 'unexpectedly lucrative,' which made a $1.16 billion deal with Amazon.com in 2012.

He was interested in sports, so in 1988, he purchased the basketball team Portland Trailblazer NBA for $70 million and later the Seattle Seahawks NFL team in 1996. Under his stewardship, the Seahawks made it to the Super Bowl three times and won Super Bowl XLVIII. He was also involved in the designing and construction of Century Link Field, an important stadium in Seattle. Ultimately, he went on to own seven sports teams.

He pursued his music interest by joining bands. A die-hard Jimi Hendrix fan, he played the rhythm guitar in a Seattle band called Grown Man, which released its first CD in the spring of 2000. Later, with his band Underthinkers, he released another album through Sony, called *Everywhere at Once*.

His interests in film and entertainment took him to Hollywood, where, through his Vulcan Productions, he made substantial investments. Some of his noted ventures here included *Far from Heaven* (2002), *Hard Candy* (2005), *Where God Left His Shoes* (2006), *Judgment Day: Intelligent Design on Trial* (2007), *This Emotional Life* (2010) and many others.

Many of his films were nominated for Golden Globes and Academy Awards. One major production of his company was *Girl Rising*, a documentary that tells the story of nine girls from nine countries who seek education. The background narrations in this film were done by major celebrities including Anne Hathaway, Cate Blanchett, Selena Gomez, Priyanka Chopra, Sushmita Sen and others.

As travel was one of his passions, he got himself

a luxury yacht, Octopus, in 2003, which, at a length of 414 ft, happens to be one of the world's largest private yachts. It was the site of his 2015 yacht party at the Cannes Film Festival, which had 'Bollywood' as the theme that year and where the guests included Natalie Portman, Antonio Banderas and Leonardo DiCaprio. It has a crew of fifty-seven and two helipads. Apart from personal use, travel and entertainment, it was also often lent out for exploratory and scientific ventures and rescue missions. In 2002, he loaned the ship to the Royal British Navy to help it retrieve the bell of the British battleship that had been sunk by the Germans in World War II. The historic bell was finally recovered with Octopus's help in 2015.

Basically a man of science, his interests in the field never waned. It's said that while Bill was a 'man of action,' Paul was a 'man of ideas'. Given his wealth, he ventured into all kinds of science and tech projects. His interests in aerospace made him fund the flight of SpaceshipOne, which was the first privately funded effort to put a civilian in suborbital space. In its flight on 4 October 2004, it was able to climb to an altitude of 377,591 ft (ten times the flight-height of commercial aircraft), and won the Ansari X Prize of $10 million. In 2011, he launched a space venture, Stratolaunch Systems, with the view to launch satellites and eventually carry humans into space. On 13 April 2019, the Stratolaunch aircraft was able to make its maiden flight, touching a height of 15,000 ft.

His philanthropic activities ranged from education to wildlife and environmental conservation, and from arts to healthcare, community service and more. He was also the founder of the Allen Institute for Brain Sciences, the Institute for Artificial Intelligence, and the Institute for Cell Science. He had committed over $2 billion for such causes.

Allen had received numerous awards and accolades and was listed among the 100 most influential men in *Times*'s editions of 2007 and 2008.

In his twenties, Allen was in a relationship with one Rita, but did not marry her then, as he thought they were too young to marry. He remained a lifelong bachelor, though in interviews he had talked of the possibility of some romantic association, which might lead to marriage.

It had been a dream run for him for about thirty years after leaving Microsoft, but in 2009, he had had a relapse of his cancer and needed to undergo treatment again. Though he had resigned from an active role in Microsoft, he had continued to be on the board of directors as he was a major shareholder of the company. However, on 9 November 2000, he resigned from the Microsoft board of directors and accepted the position of Senior Strategy Adviser to the company's executives.

Over time, whatever bitterness Paul had felt at the time of the break-up had also diminished by a great degree.

Though his 2009 relapse was cured, his disease returned in 2018 and he died of septic shock on 15 October of the same year. During his illness in 2009, Bill had visited Paul several times. Talking of Paul after his death, Bill said, 'Health had always been a major concern for him... Now as (the) children have grown up, we could have connected more often, and discuss this idea or that, but it was not to be.'

Though some of his investments and projects didn't work because of management issues, and he had seen his position slide in the rich list, in 2014, he still had 100 million Microsoft shares—and at the time of his death, he was the 44th richest man in the world with a net worth of $20.3 billion.

MOTHER MARY AND THE OTHER BILL GATES

Like my friend Warren Buffet, I feel particularly lucky to do something every day that I love to do. He calls it 'tap-dancing to work'.
— BILL GATES

Bill's Relationship with His Mother

Bill Gates's mother, Mary Maxwell Gates, was born on 5 July 1929 in Seattle to a banker father, James Willard Maxwell, and his wife Adele Thomson. Her grandfather too had been a prominent banker and was the president of the National City Bank Seattle from 1911 to 1929. After receiving a degree in Education, from the University of Washington in 1950, she married William Henry Gates Sr., a law graduate from the same university, in 1951.

After her marriage, she worked for some time as a teacher and then got involved in a range of civic and community activities. As mentioned earlier, she also served on the board of UWC. Her philanthropic work was not limited to the state, but extended to the entire county. In 1975, when Governor Daniel J. Evans appointed her to the Board of Regents to UW, she led a movement to divest the University of its holdings in South Africa to protest against apartheid. At her memorial service after her death in June 1994, then UW president, William P. Gerberding spoke of her capacity for 'infectious, effervescent joy', and her 'largeness of purpose and spirit'. He said,

> She was a luminous presence and a powerful influence at this University and in community. She was a catalyst, a person who sought and often found common ground when it was not apparent to others. Everyone trusted and respected her judgment. Her leadership was subtle, but it was steady.

Being nursed and nurtured by such a personality, it was natural for Bill Gates to have turned out to be a 'wholesome personality,' emotionally secure himself and being alive to other people's problems—a person with an 'enormous heart', as his wife Melinda would describe him. True, the mother and son had had some 'real' problems when he was growing up, and he had begun to rebel against his mother's decorum and some rigid rules at home. As the counsellor at that time had rightly suggested, they just needed to loosen their grip on him, 'let him be' and he would be alright sooner or later. Apart from some rough patches they faced, Bill bonded with both his parents well in later life.

His mother also played a significant role in helping advance his business. When Microsoft was a growing company, Bill would often accompany her on her civic assignments to companies to promote his business. In fact, as she and John Opel of IBM were together on the UWC board, it considerably helped Microsoft to establish initial association with IBM, which later proved to be a bonanza for the company.

In fact, much of the philanthropic spirit in Bill has been imbibed from his mother, as we've mentioned before, too, regarding how she always exhorted him to do more and more for others. We need to remind ourselves that that's the way she was, even much before Microsoft came into existence and the family came to be in a position to establish a large foundation.

Bill's Relationship with His Father

Bill Gates's father, William Henry Gates Sr., was born on 30 November 1925, in Bremerton, Washington, to

MOTHER MARY AND THE OTHER BILL GATES

William Henry Gates I and Lillian Elizabeth Rice. His father ran a furniture store in the town. After graduating from Bremerton High School, he enlisted in the US army and served the force for three years. After World War II, having been discharged honourably in 1946, he joined the University of Washington, earning a BA degree in 1949 and a Law degree in 1950. In 1951, he married fellow university student, Mary.

He distinguished himself in the profession, earning a lot of recognition and respect in an over four-decade-long career. He was a prominent member of the legal fraternity, widely respected and looked up to for judicious counsel. He served as the president of the Seattle King County Bar Association, and also the Washington State Bar Association. He also served on the boards of important institutions, including the Greater Seattle Chamber of Commerce. In 1995, he founded the Technology Alliance, whose mission was to expand technology-based employment in the Washington area.

We know that children don't just learn by direct teachings and parental advice; most of the learning and understanding comes by emulating people they admire and by following their idols. In other words, elders make children learn by example. As Bill had two strong role models in his vicinity, he couldn't go wrong. He has high praise for his father, whom he admired for a lot of qualities. Gates Sr. was much alive to his community and its issues, always concerned about how well it was educating the younger generation, both academically and ethically. He volunteered for a variety of social welfare activities. Bill particularly singles out his father's role in reforms and improvements in the legal system. 'The Bar was certainly the biggest thing he did,' he said. 'He had a lot of stuff about judicial reform and malpractice insurance for lawyers.'

However, being a self-made man and a self-effacing person, he always preferred to work with consensus, rather being too opinionated. According to Bill, he could've been a judge, but decided against it, as his law firm at that time was in a situation when he didn't want to leave it. 'I always thought he would be a great judge,' he said in an interview to Geekwire.com.

One major quality that Bill singles out about him is his sense of justice. 'My dad has a well-developed sense of justice,' he said. In fact, Washington as a state has one of the least-fair tax systems among all states, which puts extra burden on low-income residents. Gates Sr. led a movement, called 1098, which would have ensured greater fairness for all. He even volunteered for a bit part in a commercial where he's dunked in a tank for this. 'He was about 78 or so, and I said, "Dad, what the heck!"' Although the movement failed, Gates Sr. was satisfied at being firm in his convictions.

Gates believes his father's 'sense of judiciousness

and collaborative spirit' is very strong—the qualities he imbibed from his father, though not in full measure—as 'he has always been older than me,' he says in a lighter vein. 'He's very collaborative, very judicious, and he is serious about learning things and really knowing what he is talking about. He's good at stepping back and seeing the broad picture.'

One area where Gates's parents helped him in initial years was to help many new employees 'feel at home'. During that time, when many new people were brought in, quite a few of them were much older than Bill. 'I figured out if they were well older than me, they did a better job at connecting them into the community and whom they might want to know, and what groups they might like to be part of.'

So, in an indirect way, the family too made its contribution to the growth of the company.

LIFE AFTER MICROSOFT

*The belief that the world is getting worse,
and that we can't solve extreme poverty
and disease isn't just mistaken. It's harmful.*
—BILL GATES

Some glimpses of Gates's life, the man and the professional, have filtered through his actions and interactions in the preceding chapters. But given the personality of Bill Gates, his life story calls for a comprehensive analysis of different aspects of his life, which, even if it falls short of words to fully describe his life and times, would still afford us some idea about the magic of his unique character that has made his life so eventful.

Dedicated Professional and Entrepreneur

It's difficult to separate the personal from the professional in the case of Gates, especially in the first thirty years of his life. It appears as if destiny was guiding him towards a certain path and he just needed to follow that course. The very fact that he was able to create a marketable product at the age of seventeen and later form a company when he was only twenty, which is still one of the largest in the world, speaks volumes about him.

Some of his associates felt that, unlike other teenagers, he had missed out on his youth. Ed Roberts, the founder of MITS, the company that gave Bill Gates its first major order, once remarked, 'He's kind of like Elvis Presley. He never got to grow up.' During this time, by his own admission, he scarcely took a holiday. Sometimes, he would be up the whole night working at the office and then sleep on the floor. Once when a new secretary came on Monday morning, she found him sprawled on the floor, and she thought he was unconscious.

In the beginning, Gates would himself supervise and read every word of the code before it was shipped, and would even rewrite wherever he thought necessary. Talking of his 'busyness' those days, he said in an interview once, 'If some friend called me, I didn't have time. I was super busy. I never took a day off in my twenties. I'm still fanatical, but now I'm a little less fanatical. I play tennis. I play bridge. I spend time with my family. I drive myself around town in a normal Mercedes.'

Himself being a workaholic, Gates expected a certain degree of commitment and dedication from his staff members too. In the early days, when the company needed to keep a control over finances, he was more careful about his staff performance. By his own admission, he would even memorize the numbers of employees' car plates to keep a tab on their arrival and departure timing. There has also been much talk about his outbursts. Impatient with inadequate replies, he would burst out, 'That's the most stupid idea I've ever come across. Someone is not thinking here.' Or a sarcastic comment, 'Oh, I would think it over the weekend.'

As we've read before, Paul Allen recalls the screaming matches they had from time to time over the disagreement of certain company policies or new ventures. Gates admits that he is very hard on himself when he begins to pursue some 'stupid or unworkable idea.' 'How can I be so stupid to think of such an idea', he would muse later. However, as the company grew, Gates began to relax somewhat, and as Melinda said, has also mellowed down with age.

Intellectual Pursuits

One of Gates's childhood teachings was — stay curious. But it appears, given his basic personality, he didn't quite need it. He was inherently inclined towards looking at the world around him and wondering about it. Till today he continues to be a voracious reader, a habit that began rather too early for him. 'I read the whole set of *World Book Encyclopedias* when I was a kid', he said. His father also said that they had been quite thrilled to see that their child was so fond of reading; so much so that they had to even make a 'no reading on dinner table' rule. It is a habit that has continued. Practically interested in 'everything', he reads, by his own admission, about fifty books in a year. 'Who can read a full book on fertilizers?' asks Melinda. 'But he can.'

Fond of puzzles, one item that Gates always takes on vacation is a jigsaw puzzle. 'After I've found a home for the last piece of a puzzle, I feel refreshed and invigorated.'

Sharing his sense of curiosity and wonder with another genius of earlier times, Gates once wrote in his blog, 'When you look across all of Leonardo's many abilities and his few failings, the attribute that stands out above all else was his sense of wonder and curiosity.' He added, 'When he wanted to understand something — whether it was the flow of blood through the heart or the shape of a woodpecker's tongue — he would observe it closely, scribble down his thoughts, and then try to figure it all out.'

He was so impressed by Da Vinci's achievements that he even bought Leonardo Da Vinci's *Codex Leicester* for $30.8 million in 1994, making it one of the most expensive books ever sold. This seventy-two-page document contains Da Vinci's sketches and ideas about subjects like astronomy, mechanics, botany, mathematics and architecture. It was written between 1506 and 1510.

Bill made his mark at Harvard too, though his stay there was short. There's been much talk about the pancake-sorting problem that he solved at Harvard. The paper to this effect was published in 1979, when he was running Microsoft, titled 'Bounds for Sorting by Prefix Reversal'.

This dates back to the time when he was in second year at Harvard. This had been part of a series of unsolved problems in mathematics that Professor Harry Lewis had posed in the class. The problem was this: A chef has made pancakes of different sizes, and they need to be stacked neatly on a plate with the largest at the bottom and smallest at the top. To achieve this, first you stick the spatula under the large one at any point and flip it, with this pancake going at the top. Now in the second move, flip the whole stack and bring the large one at the bottom. Then you repeat the same procedure for the next largest one in the pile (wherever it may be), and again repeat the procedure. After a few flips, you would ultimately land up with a stack that's well-ordered, going from the largest at the bottom, to the smallest at the top.

The question was: How many flips per pancake on the upper bound would be required for the entire pile to be sorted out, whatever be the number of pancakes in the stack? It was clear that although some pancakes would require two flips each, the entire number would not require so, as in the process, others would get sorted out on their positions. It was generally shown to lie between 1.07n and 1.64n, but the exact number was not known.

Initially, Bill had worked on the problem while at Harvard, but later, in 1979, along with an assistant professor at Harvard, Christos Papadimitrious, he gave a final solution suggesting that the upper bound would be 1.67 flips each. So, for instance, we have twenty pancakes in the pile, more than thirty-three movements would not be required. This would be the upper bound. Of course you can have less flips if the number is less.

This formula was improved thirty years later by a team of researchers at the University of Texas, who established that the upper limit was 18n/11, but they did it with the help of powerful computers.

One positive fallout of 'thinking' and 'being curious' is that one begins to have all kinds of ideas about all kinds of things. And then one wants to jot them down, and then arrange them in a systematic manner. So, Bill had been doing that most of his early life, and in recent years has come out with some extremely thought-provoking books: *The Road Ahead*, published in 1995, and *Business @ the Speed of Thought,* in 1999.

Family Man

In the initial years of his business, Gates was so focused on building his company that he didn't have much time to think of romance or family. It was only when he had begun feeling secure about his business that he began to think on these lines.

Melinda caught his eye for the first time when they were sitting next to each other at a 1987 expo-trade dinner in New York. 'He was funnier than I thought,' she said. Four months into her job at Microsoft, she had had a certain impression of the boss, which was to change over time. A few weeks later, as the two bumped into each other in the company's parking lot, he asked her out. Bill being a busy man was used to scheduling his appointments and suggested a date two weeks later for going out. Melinda wondered if this hard-nosed tech genius had a romantic side to him at all, and said he should ask her near that date. Bill, intelligent as he is, got the hint and called her after an hour or two, asking if they could go out that evening. She agreed, and gradually with subsequent meetings, they began to develop fondness for each other. What struck Bill about Melinda was her forthrightness and sense of independence (she was not intimidated by the boss!). In fact, Bill would often joke in the company that his wife was more educated than him.

Melinda

Melinda Ann French was born on 15 August 1964 in Dallas, to Raymond Joseph French, an engineer and house-rentals agent, and Elaine Agnes Amerland, a home-maker. A bright student, she would generally be on top of her class in school. Her first introduction to the cyber world happened when her father brought her an Apple-II, the most popular PC those days. As her interest in computers grew, she took up computer science later and graduated in Computer Science and Economics from Duke University, North Carolina. She later joined IBM as an intern, and on the advice of her career counsellor, applied in Microsoft. She felt she had a better future with it as the company was growing. In a few years at Microsoft, she advanced from marketing manager of multimedia products to general manager of information products. She quit in 1996.

Now, after about twenty-five years of marriage, they have been able to raise three kids and lead a happy family life. Their daughter, Jennifer, was born in 1996, son Rory in 1999, and daughter Phoebe in 2002. According to Melinda, one of the secrets of their successful marriage is finding the right balance and 'balance in rights'—sense of equality. One should try to make the relationship as equal as possible and harmony would prevail. No wonder then that often the two would land up washing dishes together at night and in the bargain get quality time to discuss major family issues.

Over time, Melinda discovered that Bill not only had a romantic side, but an 'enormous heart' too. From time to time, she was able to persuade Bill to drop the children at school. That move spawned a new thinking in the other mothers at school, who exhorted their husbands to follow Bill's example. This capacity for large-heartedness has helped Bill not only in his personal dealings, but also business relationships, and has made him one of the biggest philanthropists in the world today.

Lighter, Wilder Side

Bill had been the boss of the company since age twenty, and further, he looked younger than his age.

LIFE AFTER MICROSOFT

As Microsoft began to hire, many of his new colleagues were older than him. However, in office, he needed to keep a certain decorum and a stern demeanour. This also meant that he needed to vent out his bottled-up feelings from time to time. So, if he went wild sometimes, he really can't be blamed! (After all, he was just twenty-plus!).

As the company had begun to stabilize somewhat, Bill and Paul had started feeling easy on the office front. Paul used to throw crazy Halloween parties where people went wild. He recalls that Gates got a kick out of sliding down the banister. He would run 'as fast as he could, throw himself on the banister and glide towards the kitchen.' Once, while water skiing, he had snapped his leg and needed the plaster for at least six weeks, but he showed up for skiing just after three weeks. Paul says, although his leg looked bad, it 'held up.' Often, Bill drove like a maniac (perhaps to beat the stress). Once he borrowed a friend's Porsche 928, and took it for a spin. It went out of control and crashed. Though he didn't suffer serious injuries, the car took a year to repair. In his early days at Microsoft, he had got so many speeding tickets that he had to hire an expensive lawyer to get him out of trouble.

Fond of poker, he would at times land up losing thousands of dollars in the nightly poker game in his residency hall in Harvard. Playing the game though taught him how to bluff, which came in handy later while negotiating tough business deals.

Some Work, Some Play

For the first thirty years of his life, it was all work and no play for Bill Gates. However, after the late '80s, things had begun to change, which made him begin thinking on different lines.

His business had got firmly established and he had begun to feel extremely secure about it—so much so that, in 1994, he was the richest person in the world, with a fortune of $12.9 billion.

In 1987, he first met Melinda, whom Microsoft had hired as a product manager, and Bill felt romantically inclined towards her. Their mutual attraction led to marriage in January 1994. Shortly after this, in June, Bill's mother passed away due to breast cancer. Before her marriage, she had reminded Melinda about her own convictions of 'much is expected of him, to whom much is given.'

As growth has its own problems, the US government had first initiated an inquiry into Microsoft's 'monopolistic practices', and, later, had brought the antitrust case against them. In 2000, the judge had ordered the break-up of the company in two parts, although that didn't happen eventually. All these incidents had probably taken a toll on him. Perhaps after having spent continuous years at work, a certain sense of fatigue had begun to set in.

Beginning 2000, he had started to cut down on his active role in the company. On 13 January 2000, he announced that he was stepping down as CEO to concentrate on software strategy, which meant that he sought a more 'intellectual' role compared to an involvement in the day-to-day functioning. He said he would remain chairman of the office in Redmond, Washington, while also taking the title of chief software architect. While handing over the baton to long-time friend and senior Microsoft executive Steve Ballmer, he made a break from the present.

Later in July 2008, he stepped down from an active role at Microsoft, which was the announcement of a sort of semi-retirement. It was clear that he wished to devote more time to himself, his family and the Foundation. Later in 2014, he even resigned from the position of chairman of Microsoft and took on the role of technology adviser to the new CEO, Satya Nadella. He also decided to focus more on the philanthropic projects of the Bill and Melinda Gates Foundation, and support start-ups funded by organizations like Intellectual Ventures, etc.

From then on, it was to be a different life for Bill Gates. He had begun the construction of his house in 1988, which took seven years to build and cost $63 million. It's a 50,000 sq ft, seven-bedroom house located at Medina, Washington, and has a 60 ft-long swimming pool, six kitchens, a dining hall for 200 people, and a trampoline room with a 20-ft height, besides an entrance through a private tunnel and other luxuries.

He also has numerous other properties, including a 229-acre horse farm in Rancho Paseana in Rancho Santa Fe, California, and another one at Wellington, Florida, as his daughter, Jennifer, is an avid equestrian. He also owns half of the Four Seasons hotel chain.

Opting for a more relaxed schedule compared to the Microsoft days, Bill has been taking vacations from time to time. In August 2014, he took a family vacation off the coast of Sardinia, Italy, renting a $330 million yacht for $5 million a week. It afforded him time for some real fun; first a relaxing game of tennis in the morning, and then an exhilarating water ski with his wife and children. Wanting some 'me time' off and on, he sometimes takes off to his jungle retreat, a two-storey cabin in a cedar forest in the Pacific Northeast. In 2018, he went away for a week, taking along a bundle of books and only one caretaker.

EPILOGUE

If Bill Gates is regarded as one of the greatest of our times, there are strong reasons for it. What makes him unique is that he is able to think and act differently from others—and is not afraid to do so. He has the courage and determination to strike out a new path every time. His transition—from being one of the most successful entrepreneurs and the richest man in the world to the most large-hearted philanthropists—depicts that he doesn't look at life through the prism of success or failure. It's almost as if there's an unseen power that has made him the man he is.

BIBLIOGRAPHY

Bill Gates Breaks Down 6 Moments From His Life; Wired (available at https://www.youtube.com, accessed on 26 April, 2019)

A-Teacher-Who-Changed-My-Life, Bill Gates Notes (available at http://www.gatesnotes.com, accessed on 25 April, 2019)

6 Parental Lessons That Helped Bill Gates Become a Billionaire (available at https://www.inc.com, accessed on 2 May, 2019)

A Brief History of Microsoft (available at https://www.dsp.co.uk, accessed on 28 April, 2019)

Microsoft Corporation, I History, Products and Facts (available at https://www.brittanica.com, accessed on 28 April, 2019)

Microsoft Confirms takeover of Skype (available at https://www.bbc.com, accessed on 8 May, 2019)

Computer—History of Computing (available at https://www.britannica.com, accessed on April, 28, 2019)

Microprocessor History and Brief Information about its Generations (available at https://www.elprocus.com, accessed on 1 June, 2019)

The History of Windows Operating Systems (available at https://www.webopedia.com, accessed on 22 May, 2019)

From Windows 1 to Windows 10 (available at https://www.

theguardian.com, accessed on 29 June, 2019)

Microsoft Word (available at https:// www.britannica.com, accessed on 6 June, 2019)

History & Evolution of Microsoft Office Software (available at https:// www.the windowsclub.com, accessed on 6 June, 2019)

War of the Words, *InfoWorld*, 7 February, 1994

What's Microsoft Azure (available at https://www.datamation.com, accessed on 10 June, 2019)

Microsoft Artificial Intelligence: Amplifying Human Ingenuity with Intelligent Technology (available at https://www.microsoft.com, accessed on 18 June, 2019)

Artificial Intelligence Research at Microsoft (available https://www.Microsoft.com, accessed on June 18, 2019)

Gates Deposition makes judge laugh in court (available at http://www.infoworld.com, accessed on 21 June, 2019)

A brief history of anti-piracy at Microsoft (available at https://www.zdnet.com, accessed on 22 June, 2019)

What is the Bill and Melinda Gates Foundation (available at https://www.theguardian.com, accessed on 23 June, 2019)

TIME names Bono, Bill and Melinda Gates Persons of the Year (available at www.cnn.com, accessed on June 25, 2019)

Paul Allen on Gates, Microsoft, Interview with Lesley Stahl in CBS 60 min. (available at youtube.com, accessed on 5 June, 2019)

What I loved about Paul Allen (available at https://www.gatesnotes.com, accessed on 28 May, 2019)

Allen sues Google, Apple, others over patents (available at https://www.reuters.com, accessed on 29 May 2019)

Mary Maxwell Gates (available at https://www.nndb.com, accessed on 17 June, 2019)

Bill Gates Sr. at 90: A giant impact on technology, philanthropy and the Seattle region (available at https://www.geekwire.com, accessed on 18 June, 2019)

BIBLIOGRAPHY

Melinda Gates: Being married to Bill Gates is (available at http://www.marketwatch.com, accessed on 28 June, 2019)

Office Romance: How Bill met Melinda (available at www.independent.co.uk, accessed on 3 July, 2019)

Even Bill Gates thinks he made a Mistake by not taking a Holiday in his 20s (available at https:www.scoopwhoop.com, accessed on 4 July, 2019)

Margaret Hamilton, the Woman who made Man land on the Moon, Paramita Ghosh, *Hindustan Times*, New Delhi, 14 July, 2019

MS Teases Next-Gen XBOX, 'Scarlet', Microsoft set to unveil specifications of its next-generation Xbox console at its event E3 at Los Angeles, *The Asian Age*, New Delhi, 10 June, 2019

MS warns users about malware, *The Asian Age*, New Delhi, 26 June, 2019

Alexa, I think I'm having a heart attack, New Tool lets Digital Assistants spot Cardiac Arrest and Call Paramedics, *The Times of India*, New Delhi, 20 June, 2019

MS, Intel may have fallen out, *The Asian Age*, New Delhi, 27 June, 2019

It's Official : Big Tech to face all-round Antitrust Probe, *The Times of India*, New Delhi, 5 June, 2019

AI courses a bigger draw for experienced techies, *The Times of India*, New Delhi, 21 June, 2019

AI has become so simple and affordable hat anyone can use it, *The Times of India*, New Delhi, 18 June, 2019

MS teases Dual-screen Surface Device, *The Asian Age*, New Delhi, 7 June, 2019

Software robots are taking over many manual processes, *The Times of India*, New Delhi, 9 July, 2019

Why AI makes a Good Servant, not Master, *The Times of India*, New Delhi, 31 March, 2019

Also in *The Making of the Greatest* Series

MARK ZUCKERBERG

by Abha Sharma

This is the inspiring story of Mark Zuckerberg, a young man who defied every bit of conventional wisdom to become the youngest self-made billionaire ever.

Even though controversy kept following Mark Elliot Zuckerberg from the time he created a rudimentary website for students of Harvard to rate each other, he went ahead undeterred to create the Facebook, the biggest social network in the world. Facebook has revolutionized the way people communicate, and it currently has more than two billion users worldwide. Its 'baby-faced CEO', who was depicted as a socially challenged, emotionless geek in the Oscar-winning movie, *The Social Network*, has demonstrated how to dream big and achieve it.

This biography explores the fascinating journey of Mark Zuckerberg and his many avatars—software programmer, fencing champion, Harvard dropout, founder, CEO, philanthropist, son, friend, boyfriend, husband and father.

JACK MA

by Abha Sharma

This is the incredible story of Jack Ma, who was branded as a failure but chose not to give up.

Jack Ma (born Ma Yun) studied at an ordinary institution in China and failed multiple times as a student, and yet he held on to self-belief and created the Alibaba Group, the largest e-commerce company in the world. He was rejected for more than thirty jobs, including that of a waiter, but a few years down the line, he was providing employment to millions of people. He first experienced the Internet at age thirty, but such was his business acumen that he built a company that wouldn't exist without the Internet. He learned English by talking to tourists, but he is one of the most admired public speakers in the language.

He says, 'If Jack Ma and his team can be successful, eighty per cent of the people […] can be successful.' How did Jack Ma achieve all of this in the face of constant adversity?

Get an insight into the gruelling yet amazing work culture that he built at Alibaba. Jack Ma's story has that magical capability of invoking the best in people, to inspire them to persevere and keep moving ahead, and to make them think beyond self-interest.

JEFF BEZOS

by Sangeeta Pandey

The story of Jeff Bezos, a man who redefined innovation, leadership and, of course, wealth.

This book looks at some of the defining moments and key incidents from the life of Jeffrey Preston Bezos, the world's first centibillionaire, and the journey he undertook to make Amazon the most valued company in the world.

Amazon's brilliant, visionary founder, Jeff Bezos, continues to be the driving force behind the company's astounding and continued success. From being on the verge of bankruptcy during the 1990s, Amazon is now a household name. Even after achieving so much, Jeff's passion for innovation has only increased. His new pet project—Blue Origin—aims to make space travel affordable in order to colonize other planets. Clearly, Jeff has taken the meaning of 'long-term vision' to another level.

A role model to entrepreneurs across the world, this is a man who can predict tomorrow better than anyone else.